THE
MACHINE KNITTER'S
DESIGN BOOK

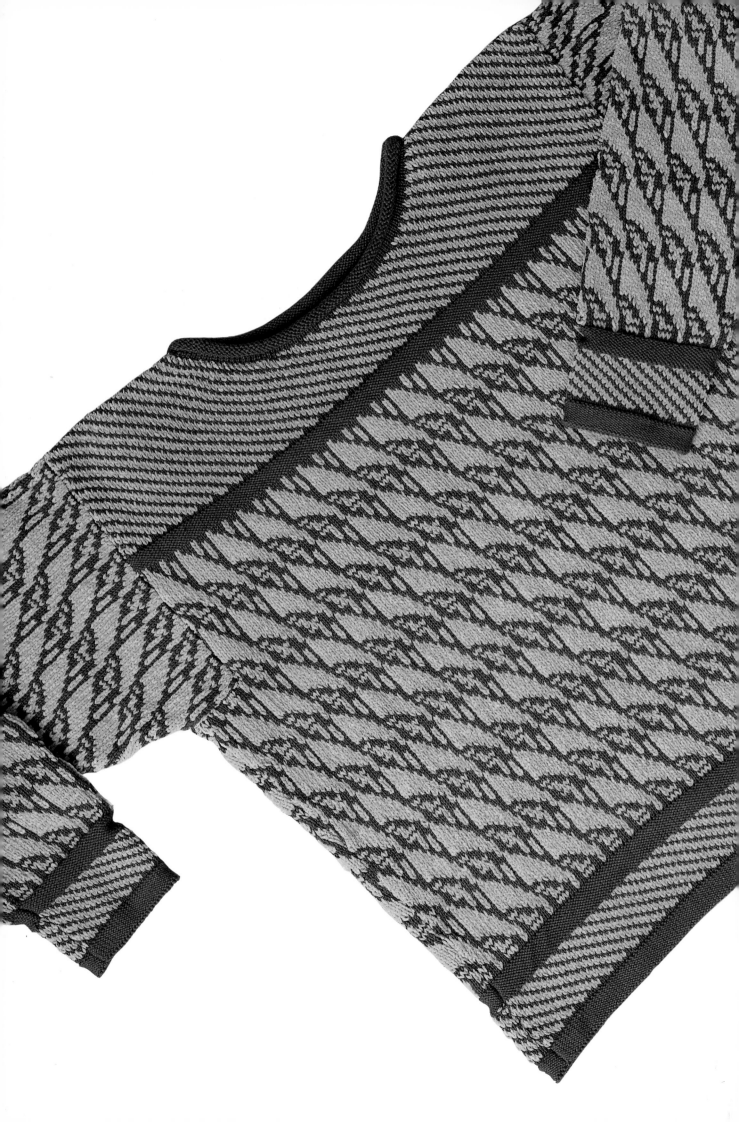

THE MACHINE KNITTER'S DESIGN BOOK

*A practical guide to creating
beautiful knitwear*

HAZEL POPE

David & Charles

ABBREVIATIONS

MY	main yarn	MT	main tension	NWP	non-working position
C	contrast yarn	4/2(eg)	MB=T4, RB=T2	EOR	every other row
WY	waste yarn	L	left	FF	fully fashioned
CO	cast on	R	right	FNR	full needle rib
COff	cast off	N(s)	needle(s)	alt	alternate
col	colour	r(s)	row(s)	in	inch(es)
MB	main bed	st(s)	stitch(es)	cm	centimetre(s)
RB	ribber bed	ss	stocking stitch	m	metre
RC	row counter	K	knit	gm	gramme(s)
carr	carriage	FI	Fair Isle	k	kilo(s)
CAR	carriage at right	HP	holding position	oz	ounce(s)
CAL	carriage at left	WP	working position	lb	pound(s)
T	tension	UWP	upper working position		

METRIC AND IMPERIAL APPROXIMATE EQUIVALENTS

LENGTH						WEIGHT	
1cm	⅜in	15cm	6in	89cm	35in	1kg	2lb 3½oz(2.2lb)
2cm	¾in	30.5cm	12in	94cm	37in	25gm	0.88oz
2.5cm	1in	61cm	24in	99cm	39in	28.4gm	1oz
5cm	2in	71cm	28in	104cm	41in		
7.5cm	3in	76cm	30in	109cm	43in		
10cm	4in	84cm	33in	112cm	44in		

Book design by Diana Knapp
Photography by Shane Edgar

A DAVID & CHARLES BOOK

Copyright © Hazel Pope 1993
First published 1993

A catalogue record for this book is available from the British Library.

ISBN 0 7153 9972 1

Typeset by Icon Graphic Services in Bembo, Bodoni and Ariston
and printed in Italy by New Interlitho SpA
for David & Charles   Brunel House   Newton Abbot   Devon

CONTENTS

INTRODUCTION

THIS IS A BOOK FOR ENTHUSIASTS; for eager beginners and experienced machine knitters alike, whose enjoyment of machine knitting nurtures a never-ending search for new stitches and techniques, new ways to use familiar ones, yarn experimentation and patterns.

A beginner wrestling with a machine instruction manual will not remain a beginner for long. The time soon comes when using the machine is second nature, and you will feel set free to be more adventurous; mastering the use of novelty yarns, incorporating more complex techniques, daring to use more expensive luxury yarns and patiently knitting more labour-intensive designs as you become engrossed in your craft. You will gain confidence to adapt existing patterns to your own preference, perhaps altering the specified yarn, or you may find yourself adapting a handknitting pattern for the machine. The more you do all this, the more you learn about the whole knitting process, and if you started out quite satisfied to follow a given pattern, you will soon arrive at the stage when you can design the whole project yourself from scratch.

You may feel that you haven't time to get too involved. Generally, machine-knitting is a hobby activity with the added bonus, or excuse, that it benefits the rest of the family and friends. As such it can be a solitary occupation, pursued for the most part by women at home. Time and opportunity to research and develop the craft is limited, and many knitters long to progress but do not know where to turn for inspiration and information. They may also feel guilty if the end product of several hours at the machine is a few interesting sample swatches, not a wearable garment. Home pressures can often require you to produce the goods rather than experiment, and though a finished garment brings its own sense of achievement, one you have designed yourself, however simple it may be, brings greater. The ultimate satisfaction in using a knitting machine lies in exploiting its technical potential to see the creative impulse through from colour and stitch combination, detail and shape to a wearable garment. Give yourself a treat and set aside time for experiment.

Inevitably a book will reflect its writer's enthusiasms, and though much of the knitting in this book can be worked on a single bed, either by option or design, writing it coincided with a growing interest in using the ribber for more than just the welts of a garment. Variations of all the ribbed stitch patterns given in the instruction book were tried, as was double-bed jacquard, following the acquisition of a double-bed colour changer. Though they were all fun to do, they did not fire the imagination as hoped. This is purely personal, they may inspire you.

Coincidentally, a much loved, well worn, bought sweater was examined to analyse the stitch technique. Black and white, obviously inspired by large and bold Aztec designs, one would have expected large floats on the reverse side of the pattern. But the reverse showed that this was not the case and, though obviously the wrong side of the garment, it was very tidy and organised, and had a charm of its own. More than that, it meant that fingers, little or large, and jewellery too, would not be caught up in strands of yarn, however roughly the sweater was pulled on. A close examination of the regularly spaced ladders running up the work showed that they had not been crocheted up, but were an integral part of the knitting. Conclusion: they must have been done on the ribber. A search through reference books confirmed this, but nowhere was there sufficient information to allow one to sit down at the machine and try out the technique, nor were there any designs using the technique and describing how to transfer from ribbed welt to what, it transpires, is known as 'ladder-backing'. The results of the research and experiments in this technique will be found in one of the patterns, as well as a single-bed technique which produces a sort of floatless 'Fair Isle'. Because it's all made so much easier by using the colour changer, it has been necessary to devote a couple of chapters to these under-used accessories, for single and double bed.

My excuse for relating the story leading up to knitting with ladder-backing is that it serves to illustrate one voyage of discovery. There are many ways of travelling, and you will have your own, bringing your own results.

There are many automatic and hand techniques shown in the samples, some of which are developed and used in the patterns. I have tried not to repeat information given in the instruction books unless I have learned or discovered a quicker or better method. It is quite a good idea to copy slavishly any technique that is new to you. Once you understand what you are doing you can bring your own ideas to bear on it, changing or developing samples as you wish. In the same way, the patterns in this book can be knitted as given, or you can change aspects of these too, using the given pattern as a starting point.

The patterns and samples have been knitted on Japanese machines. Those using the colour changer are easily worked on the Passap/Pfaff machines with Deco attachment. As more than one example of the use of each design is given, and others will suggest themselves from the samples, the pattern developments in a wide variety of yarns, stitch and detail will provide you with a springboard for your own ideas, whether for standard or chunky machine. If you find ideas and imagination in short supply, I show how I arrived at the starting point of each development, and the trials and errors encountered as I worked towards the final design and its variations. Of course you may not always agree with my conclusions, though you may find you can use some of the ideas that led to them.

I hope that my passion for yarns, knitting machines and all the accessories that go with them is infectious. Since I first learned to handknit at a very early age I have always had some sort of garment in progress. The knitting machine has extended my knitting horizons, and taught me more about yarns, stitches and patterns than I ever thought possible, becoming increasingly absorbing the more I use it.

My thanks to the machine-knitting division of Brother for their continuing support in loaning machines for the book, for help in preparing the mylar sheets, and for the patience and friendliness of their busy staff. Also for permission to use designs from *Stitchworld* in the samples. Using their machines for the garments has been a privilege, matched only by my association with the yarn suppliers: Celandine, Rowan, Texere and The Yorkshire Mohair Mill, whose gorgeous yarns make knitting an exciting business, and whose readiness to help has made the pattern knitting such a pleasure.

YARNS for Machine Knitting

ARN COMES FIRST. However interested in and fascinated you are by your knitting machine, it is a servant which manipulates the yarn for you: the yarn is the reason for the machine.

The vision of a yarn store piled high with cones of all colours and shades, types and textures has the same effect on the obsessive knitter as a lush and vibrantly lit rural view has on a romantic painter. The analogy is not overstated; many knitters will admit to a rising and uncontrollable excitement when confronted by a hoard of this wonderful stuff, often described in gourmet terms, all waiting to be transformed into equally delicious garments.

If we pause to make a simple analysis of this phenomenon, this stimulation of our creative impulse, most knitters will agree that it is colour that gets us going. Once the eye is drawn in, then the sense of touch enhances or detracts, as the yarn type and quality is assessed. We soon learn that different yarn content alters the visual impact of a colour, and that colour quality is often improved by yarn quality.

When you buy a knitting machine you open the door on an Aladdin's cave of yarns – which may soon turn into a Pandora's box for a new knitter. Everything looks wonderful, but much of the yarn is unfamiliar; some appears too fine to knit with, and there are few patterns available. Yarn selection and use go hand in hand with learning to knit, and baffle the novice quite as much as a new and unfamiliar machine.

As a teacher one collects many amusing stories, some of which are illuminating and humbling. There was the new student who turned up to a beginners' class without any yarn because she thought she was only going to be shown how the machine worked, but the knitter who brought tightly wound balls of pulled-out wool from an old handknitted cardigan was the one who taught me most. The yarn, double knitting wool, had just been unravelled. It was kinked like a tight permanent wave, knots stuck out of the rock-hard balls, and it was unusable for knitting, by hand or machine, without considerable preparation. The student's argument was that it was only for practice. Both the knitter and the tutor learned a lesson from

this. I never again assumed that a novice knitter knew anything about yarn, and now provide all-comers with light-coloured acrylic for easy introduction to the techniques. Many new knitters are not aware that there are yarns spun specially for the machine, or why these yarns should be any different from the often more familiar handknitting yarns.

HANDKNITTING YARNS

It is possible to use handknitting yarns on the machine, and indeed many machine-knitting magazines print designs for them. But because the yarn has to travel as smoothly and as quickly as possible from cone to needle through a series of mechanical controls in the tension mast, and handknitting yarns are not designed for this, they need to be prepared for this different use. First they must be wound into cones or balls on a special winder, and at the same time waxed for smooth running through the machine. The unpicked yarn mentioned above should have been wound into hanks first, which, secured against tangling, should then have been washed and dried to straighten the yarn before winding and waxing. All handknitting yarn has knots where each ball is joined, causing breakage and attendant knitting disasters, or wastage both of time and yarn when the knotted areas are pulled to the edge of the knitting to avoid jamming in the needles as they come through the tension unit. A new knitter can do without these problems, and an experienced one would not willingly court them.

Handknitting yarns are developed for the softer and more sensitive touch of hands and needles, and the more delicate ones can be spoiled by the harsher treatment meted out by the knitting mechanism of a machine. They are also, especially when bought over the counter, much more expensive than their machine counterparts, though one can raid the handknitting counter during the sales for fancy yarns for weaving on the machine. Conversely, though, many machine-designated yarns will hand-knit successfully.

There is really no need to consider handknitting yarns for general use on your machine. Aladdin's cave is full to its open doors with yarns specially spun for you, the machine knitter.

MACHINE-KNITTING YARNS

There are three main sources of supply for these yarns. The first is your local machine-knitting shop, which supplies not only yarns but also everything else that goes with the machine: all the accessories, patterns and different makes of machine, too. The second is mail order from specialist spinners, and the third is a yarn warehouse, a sort of yarn supermarket, often to be found in the most unlikely building in the most unlikely place, but this is where you will probably find the greatest variety at the lowest prices. Spinners for the garment trade, supplying yarn designed for fashion houses and multiple stores to their specification in composition and colour, often have yarns left over: ends of ranges. These would not appear in any catalogue available to the domestic knitter, but are bought up by enterprising stockists who retail often very large cones as 'industrials' at a fraction of the cost for a yarn of comparative quality from a domestic supplier's catalogue. The disadvantage is that the yarn is not repeatable, as named brands are. But though their forte is industrial yarn, these suppliers often stock a range of different brand names, which is important to the small-production professional knitter needing regular supplies of the same yarn. Conversely, you may find that your local shop stocks a limited range of industrials.

USING THE YARNS

Many knitters only feel safe knitting with a yarn marked in familiar terms – 4-ply acrylic, 4-ply Shetland, double knitting, chunky – thus knowing more or less what too expect. Patterns can easily be bought for these yarns, with quantities, tension and sizing all worked out, so there is little to worry about. But that leaves a vast area of our imaginary warehouse brimming with exciting industrial yarn marked inside the cone in unfamiliar terms. A little curiosity shows that most of these yarns are only 2-ply, as are some of the 'safe' yarns, but they vary in thickness, added to which the Shetland and a 2-ply angora may smell like a sheep pen and look like string! All very puzzling. Much de-mystification is called for.

Over recent years there has been a knitting revolution, with individual hand and machine designers setting the pace and industry hard on their heels. As a result, there has been a rapid growth of yarn supply for the domestic machine labelled in the familiar terms of handknitting, but with sufficient additional information for those who need it. For example, a good yarn from a conscientious supplier will be marked, 'Botany wool. Knits as 4-ply (or 4-ply equivalent) 3/12 worsted count. Approx 4600m/kilo'.

Dig about in a box of industrial oddments, and look inside the cones for clues. You may not see anything about 4-ply, but you should certainly see a 'fraction' of some kind. If by coincidence you saw a cone marked 3/12 worsted count, you would know what sort of yarn to expect. The 4-ply equivalent botany yarn can now join puzzle corner with the other so-called 4-plies, but lo and behold, it is 3-ply!

The first purchase of industrial yarn I made was marked 'NM 2/30 merc cotton'. 'Use three or four ends together,' I was told, so I took home four cones. There was more than enough for a sweater, but it was so cheap it didn't matter. So, as domestic machine knitters with access to industrial yarns, we need to understand some of the terms.

single, singles	A separate yarn strand
ply	A number of single yarns plied or folded together; this does *not* mean yarn thickness
fold	The same as ply
end	A specific yarn; several ends can be knitted together to make the required yarn thickness
doubling	Two or more yarns knitted together

The meaning of the 'fraction' can be complicated, but as a domestic machine knitter you do not need to know all the mathematics implied. The figure before the line refers to the number of ends, the figure after the line refers to the count. It is really not a fraction at all, though many knitters refer to it in this way.

The figure after the line is calculated from the length of yarn required for a given weight; the finer the yarn, the greater the length, and the higher the figure after the line in what is known as indirect count. So without looking, you would know that a yarn marked 2/30 would be considerably finer than one marked 2/8, though both are 2-ply.

Unfortunately, the yarn count is not standard for all yarns. The letters inside the cotton cone refer to the system which produced the count. The yarn I chose was French; NM is a continental abbreviation for metric count.

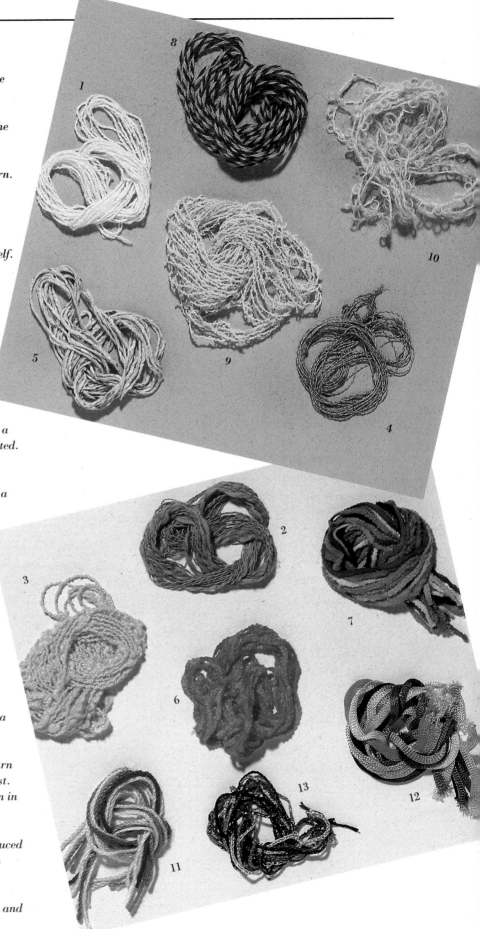

1 Cotton bouclé, showing small, tightly bound loops. Knits very well on the machine

2 Cotton slub with a viscose base yarn. The slub tends to show on the purl side of the knitted fabric

3 Combination of a slub and a bouclé yarn. The slub is the extended thick section, the bouclé the thinner, looped, section

4 Cotton knop. The yarn has been spun tightly in places so that it twists back on itself. A yarn of this weight would need ends of matching straight yarn to make a suitable knitting weight

5 Silk noil with a multi-coloured cotton nep. Noil is spun from silk waste and the resultant knitted fabric has little elasticity, so hems are better than ribbed welts

6 Chenille. Cut short ends are spun onto a base yarn to give a velvety effect when knitted. This sample is viscose

7 Chenille. This is spun in cotton, giving a less shiny but still lustrous finish

8 Marl. Any yarn containing two or more contrasting coloured ends, twisted onto a solid colour. A yarn, nearly always wool, much used for tough country sweaters

9 Snarl. This refers to small curled or kinked places in a yarn. When knitted or woven the resultant fabric has the appearance of towelling

10 Loop yarn. Here mohair is looped on a wool and nylon binder

11 The spinning technique gives crêpe yarn its characteristic smoothly interlocked twist. This sample is courtelle, but it is also spun in wool

12 Ribbon, here in viscose, but also produced in cotton and silk, and combining well with complementary yarns for special effects

13 Glitter yarn. A combination of viscose and metallised polyester

On the cover of a catalogue of regularly used Shetland yarns is the following technical information: R220T/22/8WC(2/9NM). Decoded this reads: Resultant count 220Tex/2, 2/8 worsted count, (2/9 metric count). The headache clears on reading below this the magic words: knits as 4-ply. Much of this information is irrelevant for the home knitter, and is provided for designers and manufacturers needing to calculate large quantities for production lines. A basic understanding of the count numbers is all you need if you are buying industrial yarns for your machine, and 2/8 is sufficient for you to expect a 4-ply equivalent.

YARN PREPARATION

Many natural fibres are dyed before spinning and then spun 'in oil'. Shetlands on cone are often sold with this oil left in, which gives them a stringy appearance and a distinctive sheepy odour, also darkening the colour. This was why the aforementioned angora presented a non-angora look. Thanks to the oil, it went through the knitting machine like a dream, and once washed revealed its soft and delicate nature. Washing makes a considerable difference to the measurement of the knitting, so the tension square is measured after it has been washed, dried and pressed.

If you buy a branded yarn sold specially for machine knitting, you can assume that it is ready to use. However, some knitters like to spray their cones with a wax product that is generally available, or run the yarn over a little wax disc, which is standard issue on some machines. The wax coats the yarn, controlling the fibres, and washes out easily afterwards.

YARN CONTENT

Many yarns for the machine are spun from manmade fibres, and as such are inexpensive, providing great wash-and-wear garments for the family. Their popularity continues, and they have been imaginatively developed to provide industry and the domestic knitter with exciting novelty yarns. With the rising interest in the natural yarns – wools, cotton, silk and linen – designers have ingeniously mimicked the naturals. Standards require statement of yarn content, and it is often a great surprise to find that what looks and feels like cotton, wool or mohair, reveals itself on close inspection as courtelle, acrylic, nylon or viscose. However, the true content is often apparent after a short period of wearing and washing. The synthetics are rarely as warm as the naturals, and may soon lose their natural look. Buy them for what they are. Naturals can have percentages of manmade fibre added to them to increase wearability, to reduce price or for support. Mohair is often spun onto a nylon core. Interest and sparkle can be added to natural yarns with viscose and lurex.

One needs to know the yarn content to treat a garment appropriately. A busy parent is quite likely to sacrifice warmth for wash-and-wear attributes, given that many homes, all schools and most workplaces are heated in cold weather. Natural fibres need more time and patience, though industry has produced 'superwash' wools and 'carefree' cottons in an effort to hold the market, and for those of us who want the best of both worlds and are still prepared to pay a little more for natural fibres.

YARN TYPES

When you pore over spinners' catalogues, you encounter myriad terms which describe the way the yarn has been spun and blended. Slub, knop, nep, fleck, gimp, marl: all evoke yarns that are not smooth. Yarns produced for handknitting are often given exotic names to attract the knitter. A yarn called 'Cabaret', for example, is more likely to be appropriate for evening wear than for socks and school sweaters. 'Cairngorm' would surely mean something warm and woolly. Even so, the spinners are bound by law to give a description of the yarn content alongside any romantic and evocative name they have conjured up to promote the yarn, and this will be given in percentages of the whole, but it is the industrials or the conscientious spinner who will provide the more technical description using terms familiar to the trade. Here you would find that a yarn designated 'cotton slub', for example, has sections of its length which are unspun, giving characteristic thick bulges; or one of the plies forms knotty bits – knops – where the yarn has been spun deliberately tightly so that it twists back on itself in places. For sales purposes, these technically produced effects are given enticing descriptive names, but it can be very satisfying to study this technical aspect of the textile industry as it relates to the yarns you use.

YARN SUBSTITUTION

A machine knitter has a greater production capacity than the handknitter, and the compulsion to knit

CARE SYMBOLS

WASHING

Note: The washing symbols used by yarn companies vary. Some yarns labelled with just the tub and temperature are not always machine washable. Always take care when attempting to wash any yarn by machine that is not specifically called machine washable.

DO NOT WASH BY HAND OR MACHINE

HAND

hand washable in lukewarm water only

40° C hand washable in warm water at stated temperature

MACHINE

40° C machine washable in warm water at stated temperature, cool rinse and short spin; more delicate handling

40° C machine washable in warm water at stated temperature, short spin

40° C machine washable in warm water at stated temperature

Note: 40°C = approximately 100°F

PRESSING

DO NOT PRESS

press with a cool iron

press with a warm iron

press with a hot iron

DRY CLEANING

DO NOT DRY CLEAN

may be dry cleaned with fluorocarbon or petroleum based solvents only

may be dry cleaned with perchlorethylene or fluorocarbon or petroleum based solvents

may be dry cleaned with all solutions

Note: It may be necessary to ask your dry cleaner which solutions are used to clean your knitwear.

---

may far exceed finances. An understanding of yarn will mean, among other things, that you will be able to substitute a yarn recommended in a pattern with some unnamed, and perhaps even better quality, industrial for a fraction of the price.

On the other hand, the yarn may be the springboard for a knitting idea and the search will then be for a suitable design, either one you produce yourself, or one adapted from an existing published pattern. Industrial yarns mean you can experiment very cheaply, knitting two, three or four ends together, or perhaps introducing an end of another yarn to blend in. Different stitch patterns can be tried until you arrive at the sort of harmony of yarn, stitch and colour that feels right for what you want to knit. Then you knit your tension square.

Applying the tension square to garment design is the cornerstone of successful knitting, and is fully demonstrated in Techniques. You will find the patterns helpful, too. The main pattern is always knitted in a branded yarn, but in some cases it has also been knitted in a 'find' from a box of industrial oddments, demonstrating pattern and yarn flexibility. You can follow the design through to see how I did it, and how I solved any problems that arose.

CALCULATING YARN QUANTITIES

As a non-professional knitter who does not have to calculate for hundreds of garments for production, you can make estimates based on judgement and common sense. It is very important to make notes and keep records. If you are using a branded yarn, you can always find a pattern that approximates to the style of the one you want to make and from which you can gauge the quantity of yarn you will need. Any information given in the catalogue or on the cone will further help. Weigh cones before you start to knit, and weigh them again when you have finished, noting the amount used. If you have wasted some of the yarn, and have some unusable scraps of knitting discarded around your feet, weigh those too and subtract their weight from the amount you have used. Allow for stitch patterns; tuck stitch, for example, is a notoriously greedy stitch, needing considerably more yarn than a comparative amount of stocking-stitch knitting.

If you decide to knit a complex or labour-intensive pattern – cables perhaps, or areas with hand-transfer work – don't spoil the effect and waste your time using a yarn that is nasty as well as cheap. Honour the work you put in by using something special.

TUCK and Slip

Probably the first technique you tried on your newly acquired knitting machine was a two-colour Fair Isle. If this was even minimally successful, it confirmed that you were in possession of a simple piece of equipment capable of producing complicated patterns really quickly, and gave you the incentive to explore all the automatic stitch techniques now at your fingertips.

Your instruction book illustrates each technique – Fair Isle, tuck, slip, weaving and lace – adequately enough for you to understand the way these stitch patterns work. The fun comes in playing around with colour and yarns.

*1 (Below): **Tuck stitch.** The three samples show the versatility of one stitch pattern. The main yarn knits two rows of stocking stitch; the contrast, four rows of tuck.*

In the navy and red design, two different red shades alternate in the tucking section to give a more vibrant surface.

In both woollen samples the main yarn is botany wool, the contrast is a wool/alpaca/acrylic mix.

Contrasting weight and texture can produce a dramatic knitted fabric: the glitter yarn knits the stocking stitch, 30s cotton the tucked areas and, by using the double length facility, the lightweight yarn bubbles up to give an animated surface texture. *This can be further enhanced by colour change in the tucking areas. Keep the iron away from these stitch patterns if you want to retain their special surface quality.*

The continuous strip opposite shows various examples on the same theme. A central tuck area is flanked on both sides by a variety of yarn types in harmonising colours. The shading of the main yarn either side of this uses an end of sewing cotton knitted in with the main yarn for several rows

*2 (Above): **Tuck Seed stitch.** The vertical progression of this stitch pattern imitates a fancy rib, with the colour changed every two rows. It can be used for more formal garment bands, taking into account tension differences when calculating stitch requirements*

3 **Mixing yarns and techniques.**
The stitch sequence above right was
developed for collar and cuff detail on
a suit. The slip-stitch 'rope' shows up
really well in crêpe yarn, the cream
crêpe is knitted in pattern 4 overleaf.
The scalloped edge is tucked
manually: every 6th N held for 6rs.
Then 4rs of dark contrast are knitted
to emphasise the edge, before
repeating the tuck pattern. The knitting is backed in the main yarn, a fine
industrial mohair, in stocking stitch.

4 **Blending colours.** The other two
samples demonstrate how tuck-stitch
patterns from the basic cards
provided with all machines, take on a
new life if colours are cleverly
blended. Here they are combined with
the simple 'one/one' card on a Fair
Isle setting

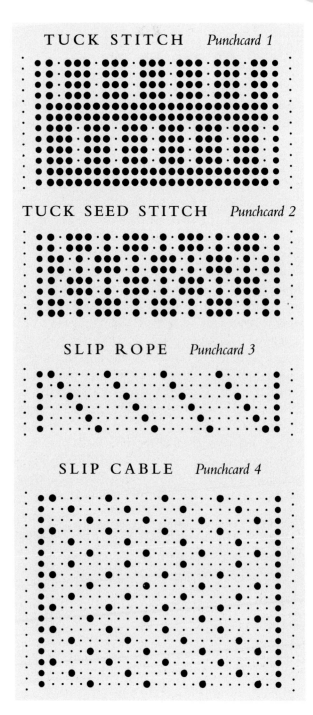

TUCK STITCH *Punchcard 1*

TUCK SEED STITCH *Punchcard 2*

SLIP ROPE *Punchcard 3*

SLIP CABLE *Punchcard 4*

In multi-coloured tuck and slip designs the colours are drawn up from one row or rows to the next. The resultant fabric has a character and surface texture totally different from the Fair Isle technique, and, of course, has no floats. At a simple level, many of the stitch patterns that come with your machine can be knitted to produce cellular fabric on a tuck setting. This is particularly useful for knitting cotton sweaters for those who need warmth but cannot tolerate wool. With the use of colour, tuck patterns can give dazzling results without floats – important for children, whose fingers catch so easily in the longer floats of Fair Isle.

Slip stitch can be organised to produce a cable effect, very attractive for trimming garments, and even more useful when knitting skirts or tops sideways. Slip stitch is also used to build up the colour in double-bed jacquard, where each colour, up to a total of four, is knitted separately in the row, the rest being slipped. It can be used in this way on the single bed too, and in both cases it is important to use fine yarn to avoid producing an inflexible, heavy fabric.

The use of slip stitch in two special ways which are great favourites of mine are explored in depth in the next two chapters. The samples shown here attempt to get the most out of the stitches at their simplest by the use of colour or contrasting yarn weights.

DOUBLE-BED JACQUARD
and the Colour Changer

A NYONE WHO HAS EVER KNITTED STRIPES or stitch patterns using several colours will know how tiresome and time-consuming it is to have to keep changing yarns in feeders and the yarn mast. A colour changer relieves you of all this labour, and streamlines the knitting action. All the necessary yarns – up to four – are threaded through the yarn tension unit and down into the changer, which is attached to the left side of the machine. Once knitting is in progress, changing colour is simply a matter of pushing the carriage up to the changer until you hear a click, and pushing the button on the changer that corresponds to the yarn colour that you want to use next. As you move your carriage back towards your knitting, the colour you have finished with returns to its feeder in the changer, and the selected colour is picked up by the yarn feeder on the carriage. Thus you can knit stripes and stitch patterns using up to four colours.

According to the make of your machine, you may have either a single- or a double-bed yarn changer, and if you do not yet have a machine it is as well to consider which type would give you the most satisfaction. If you are passionate about single-bed multicoloured tuck designs, maze and mosaic patterns which use slip and tuck technique, the single-bed changer will save an enormous amount of time. (More information is given about these stitch techniques in Chapter 4.) If double-bed jacquard intrigues you, you will get a lot of mileage out of a double-bed colour changer. Both accessories speed up and simplify the knitting of stripes and multicoloured patterns. The colour changer is sometimes known as a striper (though this generally applies to the ribbed backing pattern), and sometimes as the automatic yarn changer.

This method of feeding the yarn to the machine is an integral part of the Passap/Pfaff knitting system, eyelets holding the colours being situated at the right side of the machine where the carriage –

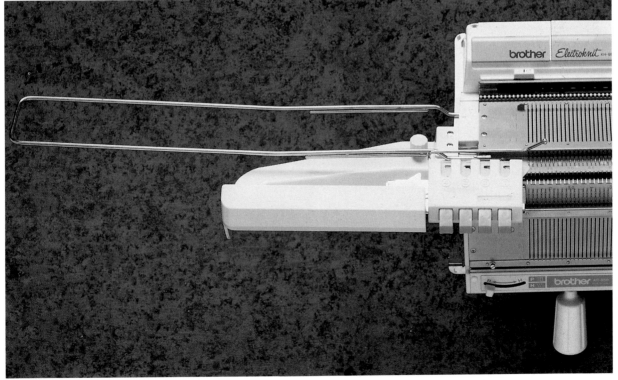

or lock, as it is termed – picks up the eyelet with the yarn required. With this, and some Japanese machines, you also have the choice of either a two-colour or four-colour facility. The four-colour changer will obviously give more service.

Many knitters assume that one can knit Fair Isle designs with more than two colours in a row using a colour changer. No domestic machine can knit more than one contrast colour per row using automatic selection on a Fair Isle setting, so the slip technique must be used to build up the colours, using one colour at a time.

Floats are the strands of yarn carried across the back of the work when knitting on a Fair Isle setting and can be troublesome if they have to be carried across more than five or six stitches. Most designers plan patterns which avoid long floats, or fill in the main design with random stitches where appropriate to the pattern.

However, it is not always possible to do this and preserve the character of the design, so if you are concerned about floats in single-bed Fair Isle, you could convert the same design for double-bed

knitting and, employing the slip technique, entirely dispense with floats at the back of the work.

Though one could change the colours every two rows by hand, this is where the colour changer, in combination with the main bed and the ribber, comes into its own. The resulting two-, three-, or four-colour design, with a ribbed backing, is known as 'double-bed jacquard'.

Most of us call multi-coloured knitting 'Fair Isle'. Everyone knows what we mean, but strictly speaking Fair Isle knitting refers to specific colours and colour designs originating from that part of the Shetlands known as Fair Isle. Perhaps the most famous of these designs is the one known as the OXO pattern.

At the beginning of the nineteenth century, a Frenchman, Joseph Marie Jacquard, patented his invention of punched cards for designs on weaving looms. These are the ancestors of the punched cards we use for needle selection on the knitting machine, and the term 'jacquard' has come to refer to all multi-coloured patterns produced in this way, including Fair Isle designs.

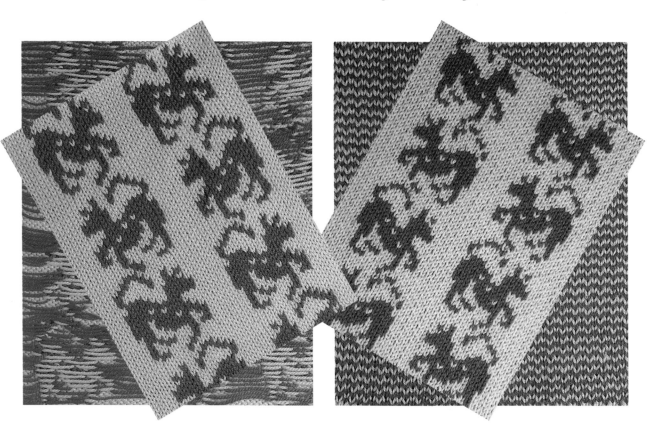

The design on the left is knitted in single-bed Fair Isle, the one on the right in double-bed jacquard. The reverse of the knitting shows the dramatic difference between the techniques. The floats on the single-bed version are far too long, making it a poor design for the single-bed machine without some alteration

DESIGNING DOUBLE-BED JACQUARD

The instruction books with all makes of colour changer show how to produce your own punchcard for double-bed jacquard. With an electronic machine, a flick of a switch is all that is needed to convert a straightforward two-colour design for single-bed Fair Isle knitting to one for knitting on both beds in full needle rib, that is, double jacquard. However, if you want to knit three- or four-colour double jacquard a mylar sheet has to be designed in the same way as a punchcard. For those with a computer in the family, there is an advanced knitting system which includes the capability to construct multi-coloured designs and load them into the knitting machine ready to knit.

Once one has understood the structure of a two-colour card, adding a third and perhaps a fourth colour will be a logical progression when you want a multi-coloured design.

THE DOUBLE-JACQUARD PUNCHCARD

Remember that you are using the slip-stitch technique. Selected needles will knit, non-selected needles will slip. You will knit two rows in main, or background yarn, then two rows in contrast throughout. As one row is knitted, the needles for the next row on the main bed are selected.

The ribber needles knit on every row, though they can be set to slip in one direction. The colour changer is at the left side of the machine, the card locked on the first, background row, knitted in main colour. The carriage is at the left, set to select the pattern. Knit to the right. Release the card, and knit to the left. The background needles that were selected on the previous row have knitted, and the contrast needles have been selected for the next row. If you watch closely as you do this you will soon understand how the pattern is built up. It can be summarised as follows:

r1,MY Background is knitted, background Ns are selected. (Card is released at beginning of pattern.)

r2,MY Background is knitted, contrast Ns are selected.

r3,C Contrast is knitted, contrast Ns are selected.

r4,C Contrast is knitted, background is selected.

r5,MY Background is knitted, background Ns are selected.

r6,MY Background is knitted, contrast Ns are selected.

From this you will see that, because you knit the main yarn for the background and then the contrast, two passes of the carriage are necessary to produce one row of knitting, so if you have a sweater requiring 180 rows from waist to shoulder, the row counter would register 360.

The African Weave design in the pattern section of this book is knitted using a form of the double-jacquard technique. The design is drawn out for the mylar sheet, and also for the punchcard. A comparison of the two studied in conjunction with the analysis of the structure given above should help you to understand what is happening. If you find it difficult to understand, knit some samples of the pattern cards that come with the colour changer. Once you have the feel of the equipment, watch what happens as you knit the fabric.

When you feel bold enough to design for more than one contrast colour, you will see that rows 3 and 4 above would be knitted in your first contrast, rows 5 and 6 in contrast 2, rows 7 and 8 in contrast 3.

MAKING YOUR OWN DOUBLE-JAQUARD PUNCHCARD

Your instruction books will tell you how to do this, but Mary Weaver's explanation in *The Ribbing Attachment* Part 2, gains top marks for clarity. She refers to the design area as 'positive', the background as 'negative'.

If you are using a punchcard blank, you will have the two fully punched rows at either end for the overlap when joining the card. If you are using a continuous roll from which you cut whatever you need, you will have to punch a double row first, and again when the design is finished. (These rows are not shown in the illustrations.)

- Mark in the **positive** rows first:
- Starting on the second row of a blank card, mark in with a soft pencil the first row of your design.
- On the next row mark in your second row.
- Miss two rows.
- Mark in the next two rows of your design.
- Miss two rows.
- Continue like this to the end of your design.
- Check that you have two blank rows alternating with two punched pattern rows, with one blank

row at the beginning and one at the end of the pattern, before punching out the design.

- Mark in the **negative** (background) rows:
- On the single blank row at the bottom of the card, mark all the holes which were not punched on the row above.
- On the first of the next pair of blank rows, mark all the holes which were not punched on the row below.
- On the second, mark all the holes which were not punched on the row above.
- Continue to the last single unpunched row which follows the last pair of positive rows.
- Mark in the holes which were not punched in the row below.
- Finish by punching out two rows for the overlap if this is necessary.

The manufacturers either provide you with, or show you how to make, a check card. This has rows 2 and 3, 6 and 7, 10 and 11, and so on, coloured. If you lay this beneath your card after

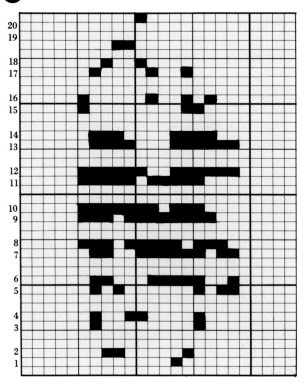

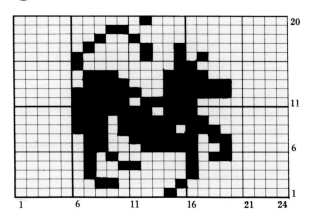

1 The basic design, using the 'little dog' motif originally developed for use in a sweater combining Fair Isle and cable

2 The contrast, or positive, rows are marked in for the punchcard motif

3 The background, or negative, rows are marked in on the punchcard. They are knitted in the main or background colour. The directional arrows apply to the colour changer. If working without one, the knitting direction is reversed

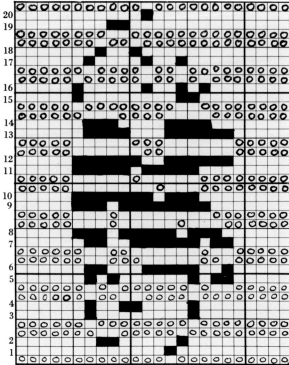

punching out the positive rows, the colour shows through, and will reveal any mistake you have made in row order.

THE KNITTED FABRIC

The instruction books for the ribber and double-bed colour changer are only an introduction to rib jacquard, and once you have grasped how the fabric is constructed, you will see that the backing, formed on the ribber, can have an attraction of its own. You will want to try out all the different ribber settings given and assess how they affect the face and the reverse of the knitting, as well as its handling quality or 'feel' – the knitted fabric produced in this way is distinctly machine made, and bears no relation to any handknitted stitch as do so many of the single-bed stitch patterns.

For the fabric to feel soft and fluid, as good knitting should, it's important to use a fairly fine, soft yarn. Many of the industrial yarns perform well, knitting up smoothly and, though good and inexpensive to practise with, will produce garments that reflect what they cost. If you have spent time and care on devising a design and have confidence in your knitting technique, a little extra money spent on a special yarn will produce a garment worth all the thought and care invested in it. Using woollen yarn, a worsted count of 2/16 or 3/16 should give a soft feel to the knitting, and can be combined with fancy yarns of the same weight and quality.

LADDER-BACKED JACQUARD

There is a compromise technique using the jacquard card which allows you to design and knit patterns without using a full needle rib. This can conveniently be called 'ladder-backed' jacquard, for obvious reasons.

For this technique all the needles on the main, or back, bed of the machine are in working position, but only selected needles on the ribber. This means that any floats which might have been too long when the design is knitted as single-bed Fair Isle are caught and knitted by the ribber, producing an attractive ladder effect at the back of the work. These needles can either be set in a regular grouping, having every 4th needle on the ribber in working position, for example, or, as a slight division appears on the front of the work wherever the ribber needles are in use, they can be used to emphasise a design. To do this, the ribber needles are plotted across the bed in relation to the pattern

position, and brought into working position for this emphasis.

Because one is not knitting a full needle rib, the work is less solid, so thicker yarns can be used than for any of the other jacquard settings. This attractive technique is used in the African Weave sweaters on page 72, not only because it is a great favourite, but because it seems to be thought of as a 'poor relation' and only worth a brief mention in instruction books, the details of its use not being fully discussed.

The general instructions that follow apply to all machines, including the chunkies. While the technique is possible without a colour changer it is, of course, more laborious.

WORKING LADDER-BACKED JACQUARD

When you have worked your garment rib, the needles must be arranged so that only those selected for the backing remain on the ribber. How you do this will depend on the kind of rib you have knitted, and whether you want to increase the number of stitches for the main part of the work.

If you are not increasing, bring up the empty needles on the back bed to working position, and transfer the unwanted ribber stitches onto these. Observe the needle rule for your machine. This may mean that whatever needle arrangement you have planned for the ribber will not be maintained at the edge of the work. This does not matter, the needle rule is more important.

If you are increasing the number of stitches for the main part of the work, all the ribber stitches need to be transferred to the main bed. These are then knitted onto waste yarn and the work removed from the machine. The extra needles you need for the increase are brought to working position, and the work is then rehung, making the increases evenly across the knitting (see Techniques).

Now set the half-pitch lever to H, so that the ribber needles are opposite the sinkers of the main bed.

Select the ribber needles. If no vertical emphasis to the pattern is required, observe the needle rule for your machine and push ribber needles to working position at regular intervals across the machine bed. Now, using the double eyelet tool, pick up the heel of each main bed stitch that most nearly corresponds to the ribber needle opposite it, and transfer it to this needle.

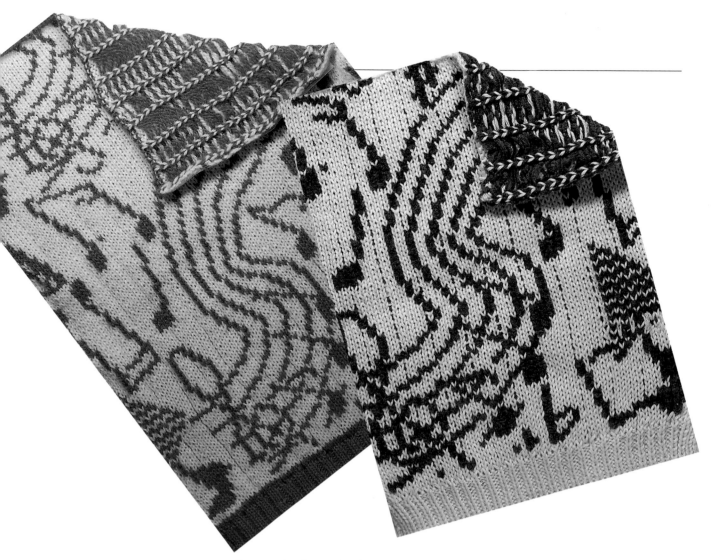

Two samples from a familiar Brother design for Fair Isle, here knitted in ladder-backed jacquard. Acrylic yarn is used for the one on the left, the other is in cotton with chenille as the contrast – a very good yarn combination for this technique

EMPHASISING THE PATTERN

To emphasise the pattern on the main bed, you need to know where it occurs in relation to the needles.

Punchcard machines

The front rail is marked in sets of 24 stitches. These needles show where the pattern on the card repeats across the needle bed.

Starting with the centre 24 stitches on the main bed, select those needles on the ribber you need for pattern emphasis. (The half-pitch lever is still on H.) If your pattern starts at N12 to the left of centre O, the ribber needle that needs to be in working position is to the left of this: N13. N12 to the right of centre O on the main bed will be matched by N13 on the ribber. You can then arrange the needles where necessary for emphasis within the centre 24st repeat. Repeat each 24st group across the bed to left and right from the centre.

Electronic machines

Patterns with an even number of stitches centre at O, having an even number of stitches at either side. Patterns with an odd number of stitches centre on N1 to the right of centre O. For example, a 15st repeat would run from N7 at the left to N8 at the right. The ribber needles are then set in the same way as for punchcard machines.

A FEW POINTS

Remember to fit the fine-knit bar – sometimes called the close-knit bar – to the machine as instructed, and to have it in place when you knit your tension square. Its function is to raise the needles slightly to ensure that the finer yarn is knitted off the needles properly. If you have forgotten to put it in before knitting the welt, it can be inserted with knitting already on the machine. However, it will alter the tension slightly, so do not insert it halfway up a garment piece. Remember to knit all garment pieces in the same manner.

The ribber tension should be set approximately two whole numbers lower than main tension.

Set the ribber to knit in one direction, and slip in the other for ladder-backing. This reduces the number of rows knitted on the ribber and so lightens the fabric. If you find that you regularly lose stitches on either bed with the ribber carriage set like this, then setting it to knit both ways, though not ideal, should solve the problem.

Being inflexible, cotton often misbehaves in this way, but it is worth trying samples on various settings before making a decision. Remember, the ribber is knitting on every row, and the back bed, with the carriage set to slip, needs two passes to knit one row, so you will have twice as many rows on the back of your work if you do not set the ribber carriage to slip in one direction.

All these points also apply to chunky machines. The double-bed colour changer produces a very good fabric when used with the chunky machine on the ladder-back setting, where patterns worked in single-bed Fair Isle would have long floats. This can distort the face of the knitting, and cause inconvenience in wearing.

If you have not used your ribber for much more than welts and neck bands up to now, give yourself time to become really familiar with it before you embark on designing for yourself in this technique. You should also become familiar with the technique known as 'cut and sew'. This is by far the easiest way to work necklines when knitting any form of double jacquard. You will find details for working this given in Techniques and in the relevant patterns; it is much easier than it sounds, and gives a wonderfully neat, professional finish to a garment.

These two samples show how a design with a strong vertical theme can be emphasised using the ladder-backed technique. The sample on the left is knitted in single-bed Fair Isle; the floats are really too long to be acceptable. The sample on the right has every fifth needle working on the ribber. This knits in the floats and delineates the verticals

4

SINGLE-BED SLIP-STITCH
and the Colour Changer

IN MY CUPBOARD HANGS a three-quarter length jacket, handknitted in grey crêpe wool. It has pockets and, instead of a collar, a long, long scarf evenly knitted in garter stitch, the ends shaped on the diagonal, and fringed in black.

It was knitted by my mother, whose passion for handknitting went hand-in-hand with an instinct for economy; the design was chosen not only because it was stylish (it still is, after thirty years), but also because it would take a long time to knit. Her passion for wool and needles exceeded the money she was prepared or could afford to spend, and those cardigans, jackets and jumpers that were not knitted from recycled or sale-purchased yarn were knitted in intricate stitch patterns. The knitting grew slowly, even in the hands of an expert; as it grew it warmed the knees, a further contribution to the economy of a non-centrally heated north-country household!

The fabric of the jacket has a firm texture obtained by a combination of knit and slip and garter stitch. It was always known as my 'knitted tweed jacket', and evoked comments, proudly received, that it was more like woven coat material than knitting. While the craze lasted, several smart and fashionable garments were produced in two, three and four colours, using this technique, though I myself can only claim to have finished one. I

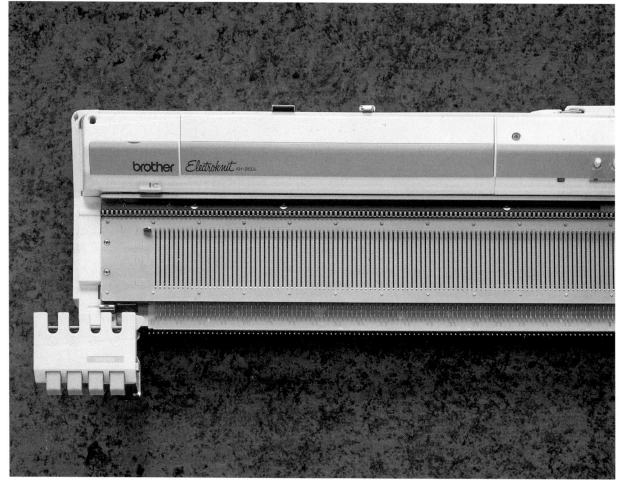

Picture courtesy of Brother Machines

remember the pattern exhorted me to: 'knit this fashionable jacket in birdseye tweed'. The instructions for these stitch designs were written row by row. The knitter, with no close-up of the stitch to go by, had to follow these and see them materialise as the knitting grew.

The instruction book for the first knitting machine I owned showed me stitch patterns using tuck and slip technique producing patterns very similar to the handknitted ones I was familiar with, though without the garter-stitch texture. At about the same time I was given a book, an American publication, called *Charted Knitting Designs* by Barbara Walker. Here I found a chapter devoted to 'mosaic' patterns, a more accurate description of our 'knitted tweed' patterns. Furthermore, the charts proved much easier to work from than the line-by-line instructions and, though a few samples were tried out of interest, the speed of knitting similar designs on the machine was more attractive, and I soon found it possible to adapt the charts for the machine.

Machine instruction books give colour illustrations of multi-coloured tuck and slip designs. These show that the disposition of the slipped or tucked stitch combined with regular changes of colour produces a kind of false Fair Isle. The way the stitch behaves draws colour from one row into the next and can give the impression of more than one colour in the row. Of course there are no floats as there are in Fair Isle, so it is often called 'floatless Fair Isle'.

It is this aspect of the knitting that commends itself to knitters; a fabric is produced which is colourful, soft and flexible, having the bonus of a certain amount of surface texture, knitted on the main bed only, but with no floats for fingers to catch on. As such it is invaluable for children's clothes, and for those of us who pull our clothes on rather less carefully than we should. Many of the designs, being neat and small, are appropriate in scale for small garments. Geometric and mosaic-like stitch patterns are the special characteristics of slipped and tucked stitch designs.

THE PATTERN STRUCTURE

Remember that, when you knit in slip or tuck stitch using punchcard or mylar sheet, the machine will knit stocking stitch on selected needles – it is the unselected ones which will pattern. If you look at pre-punched cards or the charts for the memorised patterns, you will see that it is the background

which is punched or blacked out and the design shows in the blank squares. These are the stitches which will be slipped or tucked. Though not all slipped or tucked patterns are worked in pairs of identical rows, the 'mosaic' type designs we are dealing with here call for two rows main colour, two rows background.

Electronic machine owners can use the negative button or switch to relieve the tedium of marking all the background stitches. Punchcard knitters will need to punch out the unmarked area of their card. The extra labour of punching every row twice can, however, be avoided, as most punchcard machines have a double-length or pattern-elongation lever. All electronics have this facility.

The samples developed in this chapter use the slipped-stitch technique to produce mosaic designs, showing a true harmony between design and the technique used to produce it. In designs of this nature the slipped stitches create the vertical progression of the pattern, and are isolated between stocking-stitch areas which give horizontal stripes of colour. As each row is knitted twice, the knitting chart will be in proportion if it is drawn on squared graph paper, and not on a stitch-related graph paper. Thus one square will represent one stitch, but two rows. After the slipped stitches are plotted on the design, it is easily transferred to the punchcard. Electronic owners will find it easier to redraw the knitting chart on the graph paper which comes with their machine, so that the design can be traced onto the mylar sheet.

FROM DESIGN TO KNITTING CHART

As well as a card punch, blank punchcards or blank mylar sheet and appropriate marker, you will need graph paper marked in regular squares, a soft pencil – say a 3B or even softer – and a rubber. A putty rubber is best because you can squeeze it to any shape you want, and this is useful for rubbing out single squares as you make your design. You will also need a red fibre point, or similar pen.

On the original pattern the black squares will represent the design knitted in contrast colour; the white squares the background, knitted in main colour. Each square will represent one stitch, but two rows. Horizontal lines of either design or background can be any convenient width but no more than two rows tall. The verticals should be only one stitch wide, but can be as many rows tall as necessary for the design.

Choose any of these grids to plan your design according to the sort of background you prefer: horizontal or vertical stripes, alternating or plain birdseye

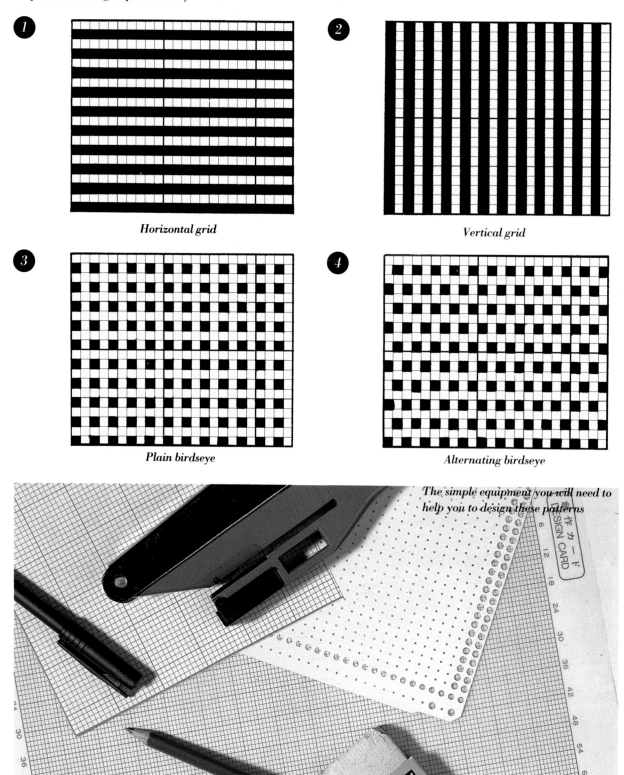

1 Horizontal grid

2 Vertical grid

3 Plain birdseye

4 Alternating birdseye

The simple equipment you will need to help you to design these patterns

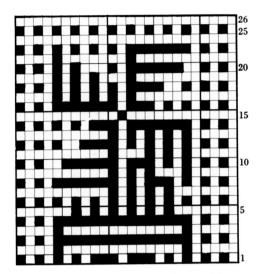

***Windmill**, 24sts×26rs planned on grid 3*

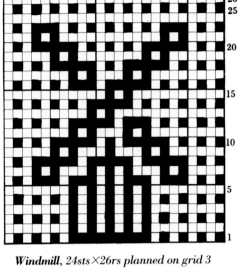

***Windmill**, 24sts×26rs planned on grid 3*

***Little Bird**, 24sts×20rs planned on grid 4*

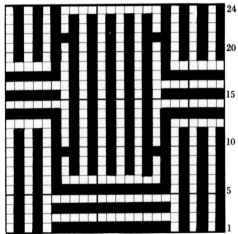

***Basketweave**, 24sts×24rs planned on grid 1 or 2*

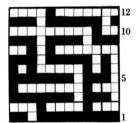

***Small Maze**, 12sts×12rs planned on grid 1. This gives an interesting diagonal effect*

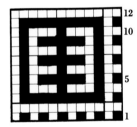

***Mosaic 1**, 12sts×12rs planned on grid 1. Repeat r1 for an edging*

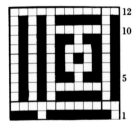

***Mosaic 2**, 12sts×12rs planned on grid 1. A more open design than Mosaic 1*

Planned on the grids opposite, single slipped stitches are flanked by non-patterning stitches. Main colour (background) is slipped on contrast rows, contrast slipped on main colour rows. Each row number on the right represents a pair of rows

The stitches to be slipped are marked in on the pattern with a 'V', the international symbol for a slipped stitch.
Then they are transferred to punchcard or mylar sheet.

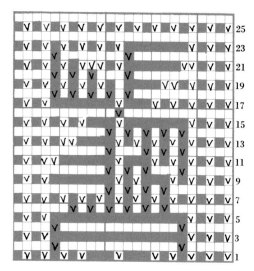

Windmill 1 24sts×52rs. You can see where the rules have been broken and two or three slip stitches are adjacent

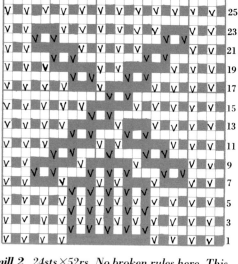

Windmill 2 24sts×52rs. No broken rules here. This design has been counterchanged in a sample in the pattern section (p114)

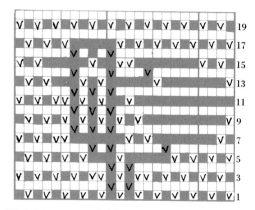

Little Bird 24sts×40rs. Odd rows are knitted in main colour, even rows in background colour. Main colour rows have single background stitches and can have blocks of main colour stitches.
Background rows: single main stitches, blocks of background stitches

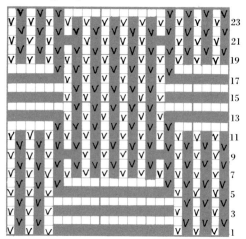

Basketweaves 24sts×48rs. Horizontal bands of stocking stitch can distort the fabric, this is remedied by pressing

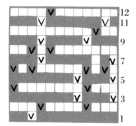

Small Maze, 12sts×24rs. This design was planned to look like a maze. The overall diagonal effect was a pleasant surprise

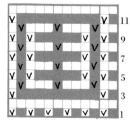

Mosaic 1, 12sts×24rs. A simple square design, suitable for an edging if r1 is repeated

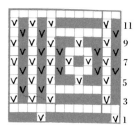

Mosaic 2, 12sts×24rs. A variation on the square. A less rigid pattern than Mosaic 1 when used as an all-over design

To create a design which is easily translated to a working chart, first prepare a grid on the graph paper. This can either show alternating horizontal rows of contrast and background (main) colour, or alternating vertical stitches. On the horizontal chart, shade in with pencil all the odd-numbered rows, ending with an even, blank row; on the vertical, shade in alternate columns of stitches starting from the first on the right. You can then rub out single shaded squares and shade in single blank squares to produce a distinctive slip pattern. The pattern is planned so that single slip stitches, or groups of alternating single slip stitches, are flanked by blocks of non-patterning stitches. The non-patterning stitches will be in contrast colour on odd rows, in main colour on even rows. A glance at the diagrams on page 26 should clarify this. The design is planned so that not more than one stitch will be slipped at a time.

It is possible to produce formal figurative designs based on suitably shaped subjects such as fruit, houses, trees, – in fact anything that can be simplified into a distinctive, positive silhouette which can then be opened up with regularly placed slipped stitches. Two kinds of grid can be prepared for this type of design, depending on the background patterning. On the first row and every following alternate row, the same alternate stitches can be shaded, as shown in diagram 3, page 26. Or the shaded stitch can also be alternated, as shown in diagram 4.

The bird and the two windmills are examples of these grid plans. The rules have been bent a little on these designs; there are two slipped stitches next to each other in unavoidable places.

In the bird design the original grid is plotted with the shaded stitches alternating overall. The design is kept as simple as possible. To remind you: on rows where shaded stitches occur, all the blank squares represent slip stitches. On the unshaded rows, single slip stitches are shaded in where necessary.

The rows are numbered on the right. The numbers represent pairs of rows: two rows of contrast colour; two rows of main.

NOTE

On the punchcard it is the background you will punch, NOT the marked stiches. Electronic machines use the negative button or switch to select the background needles. The small motifs are quick and easy to design and are a good introduction to the technique

WINDMILL 1 *Punchcard*

The first windmill design transferred to the punchcard, ready to knit. The slip stitches were marked in, but the background was punched out

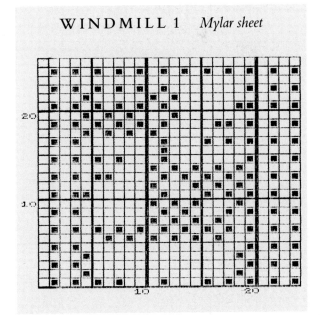

WINDMILL 1 *Mylar sheet*

The same slip-stitch design marked on the mylar sheet. The slip stitches are marked in, and the negative switch is used when patterning

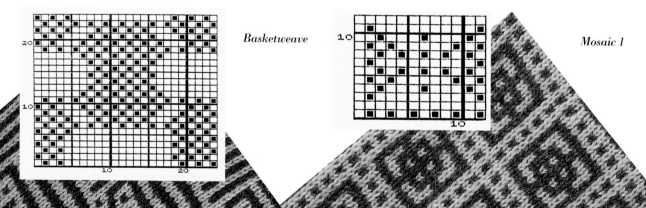

The punchcard and mylar sheet for this Windmill design appear on the previous page, showing designs prepared for different systems of patterning. The remaining patterns are all shown prepared on the mylar sheet for the electronic. Electronic knitters will use the negative button or switch, punchcard users need to punch out the background and, of course, to prepare a card with a minimum of 32 rows. Both systems need to be elongated so that each row is knitted twice.

The Windmills have been counterchanged using the facilities of the electronic, the Little Bird has also been reversed on alternate repeats. The resulting design was used for one of the sweaters in the patterns (p114), drawn out for use with either punchcard or electronic machine

Windmill 1

MARKING IN THE SLIP STITCHES

Remembering that on the odd, shaded rows it is the blank squares that denote stitches to be slipped, and the single shaded squares on the even rows, all the stitches to be slipped are marked in as a V with a red pen. This gives the chart from which we can knit. All that is needed now is to copy this onto a punchcard or mylar sheet. Remember that the last blank row is part of the design. Remember it is the unmarked, background areas you will punch out on a punchcard. Remember also to use the negative button or switch on the electronics, and on both punchcard and electronic machines remember to use elongation.

KNITTING TENSION AND THE TENSION SQUARE

You will need to experiment with tension to give you the quality of fabric you want. Tension 6, using 2/21 count Shetland yarn is a little firm, but most of these samples were knitted like this. A softer result which is more comfortable to wear was obtained using an unmarked main yarn from an oddment sale with a botany yarn, or even better, an acrylic/wool/alpaca mixture. One of the samples was knitted on tension 10 by mistake, using the Shetland yarn, and proved that, though 10 may be a little extreme, a looser tension would give a more sympathetic fabric.

The tension square is knitted in the normal way. The whole square must be knitted in pattern, not just the area to be measured, but knit the contrast rows in stocking stitch.

GARMENT PLANNING

It is sensible to keep the garment shape as simple as possible, and many knitters use the cut-and-sew technique for necklines, especially when using a colour changer. Slip stitch needs more rows and stitches to a 10cm/4in square than a comparative stocking-stitch area, and the increases and decreases will therefore have a greater number of rows between them. If you do not feel confident, it would be sensible to knit a small practice neckline in scrap yarn before embarking on a final design, perhaps in expensive yarn. You will find more

Basketweave

Mosaic 1

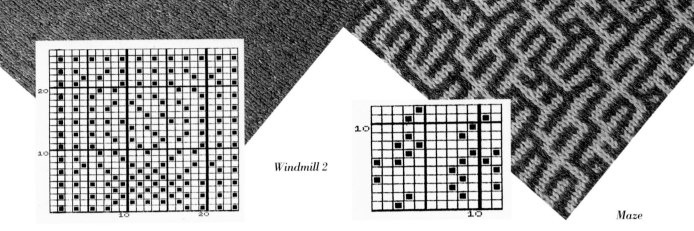

Windmill 2

Maze

comments about this in the planning of the slip-stitch sweaters in the pattern section (p114).

THE SINGLE-BED COLOUR CHANGER

It is simple to knit these slip-stitch designs without a colour changer; the change of yarn is done at the right side of the machine, and though it is a tedious job, it is surprising how soon the whole thing picks up speed, particularly if there are only two colours involved. So if you think that you will not use the technique very often, a single-bed colour changer may not be at the top of your 'wanted' list. However, it would also facilitate the knitting of multi-coloured tuck, stripes and Fair Isle designs up to four colours, so it would prove itself useful.

The colours are changed in exactly the same way as for the double-bed changer. If you decide to shape the neckline on the machine, work the left side first (this applies to all stitch techniques). For our mosaic designs, the first row of the pattern is memorised from right to left, using the background colour, or with no yarn in the feeder and the carriage set to slip. Then the first two rows will be knitted in the colour chosen for the design.

INSPIRATION

Inspiration for these designs can be found in books about Celtic ornament, traditional Japanese designs for printed cloth, Arabic designs, designs for carpets (particularly Kelims), Aztec and Mayan designs – the scope is enormous. Many of these designs reflect the necessity to formalise natural forms and to produce regular patterns.

If you have designed your own pattern, it is an exciting moment when you take the first knitted sample off the machine and find it has knitted up exactly as you had planned. It is advisable to draw the original design in a block of nine repeats to gain an overall impression, and to check that the design is repeating correctly. Small repeats may be checked without these precautions, and with single units such as the windmill or the bird you only need to make sure that you have enough background pattern to separate each repetition. You will find developments and combinations of the designs shown here in the pattern section, but you will gain greater satisfaction in producing mosaic designs of your own once you have understood how these little designs were constructed.

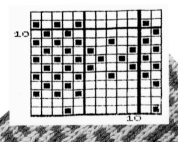

Mosaic 2

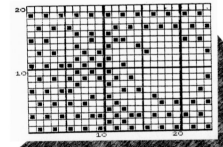

Little Bird

5

HANDWORKED *Techniques*

As AN ENTHUSIASTIC CONVERT to machine knitting, seduced by the newly discovered speed, it was some time before I considered working cables or simple lace designs by hand. The love of handknitting returned, and for that I reserved the complex stitch patterns associated with traditional Aran designs and their modern variations. I very much missed the depth of texture these designs produced, derived, as many of them are, from bas-relief sculpture.

When the first non-automatic chunky machines appeared it was impossible to do anything other than simple stocking stitch without manually organising needles and yarn. Very soon it became obvious that this was a machine ideally suited to handworked patterns that were not simply slowly achieved imitations of the automatic standard machine. The non-automatic machine drove me to explore cables, especially when worked in combination with the ribber, open transferred stitch patterns and, of course, intarsia. Though time consuming, the knitting was absorbing, and the work grew very quickly on the chunky machine. The designs were easily planned on graph paper, and because the stitch symbols are the same (with very few exceptions) for machine and handknitting, and are international, they had a wider application.

Of course it takes longer than the many clever techniques the automatic and electronic machines can conjure up, but still only a fraction of the time required to knit the same thing by hand. And, in defiance of electronics, I graduated to cables and transferred stitch patterns onto the standard machine, too. Patterns nowadays are often a highly successful mix of techniques: cables with lace, cables with Fair Isle, cables with garter stitch, and sometimes a little bit of everything, giving a richly textured and really interesting garment.

It is important to make sure that one is not laboriously handworking a stitch pattern that the machine can produce automatically. Many swung ribs shown in the ribber handbook are a good compromise if you are searching for surface interest on the knitted fabric, and most standard machines have the facility for lace, so you would probably only hand transfer this on a chunky machine without the lace-making facility.

If you want to combine lace with rib you will have to hand transfer. It is surprising how quickly the knitting chart impresses itself on the memory, and how deft and quick one becomes with the transfer tool. The standard machines are happy to knit double-knitting weight yarn on a tension of 8 or 9 if you want your work to grow quickly. All the samples here were worked in double knitting, 4/9½ worsted count, 2,700 m/kilo. Some samples are developed in Combining Techniques (p42) and in the patterns (pp62-122). Intarsia is described with the pattern on page 93.

· · · · · · · · · · · ·

LITTLE BELLS

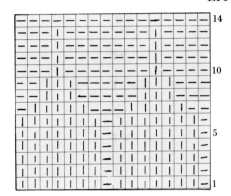

Planned as a potential collar, the tensions of this sample are graded to control the lie of the knitted fabric to make it curve. It can easily be knitted using the garter carriage, but here is worked by transferring stitches from one bed to the other using the double-ended transfer tool from the ribber accessories.

CO 1×1 rib, multiples of 8sts, plus 1. K T4/4 for several rs ending CAR. Transfer the sts so that the first and last st are on the MB, the rest as chart. Follow the chart, altering the tension as follows: rs1-6, T5/7; rs7-9, T7/5; rs10/11, T8/5; rs12, 13, T9/5; r14, T10. COff loosely behind sinkers using a transfer tool

MAKING CABLE TRANSFERS

Cable transfers are generally made on the main bed. Remember that you are looking at the back of the work, so the direction of the transfer on the purl side is the opposite of what you will see on the right, knit side, of the work. Make sure the stitches waiting to be transferred sit well down on the transfer tool. If possible, hang the transfer tool on the needles to one side of the work, or hold the tool against the knitting with one hand while you transfer the balance of the stitches to the new needles.

This chart shows the needle set-up and stitch transfer for the double-bed cables. For the single-bed cables it is virtually the same, the two knit stitches representing one needle out of work

Three cross three is about the maximum width for a machine-knitted cable. Larger transfers can be made by using short rows (see Techniques).

Yarn choice also influences flexibility. Wool and wool mixtures have elasticity because of the structure of the woollen fibre, whereas cotton, linen, silk and most manmade fibres are quite the opposite. This not only makes the crossing difficult, but puts a strain on the needles when the next row is knitted. In any case, this row should be knitted with care, if possible bringing the needles with the cable stitches out to holding position before knitting them back. The samples are worked in lightweight double knitting wool, 4/9½ worsted count on a standard gauge machine.

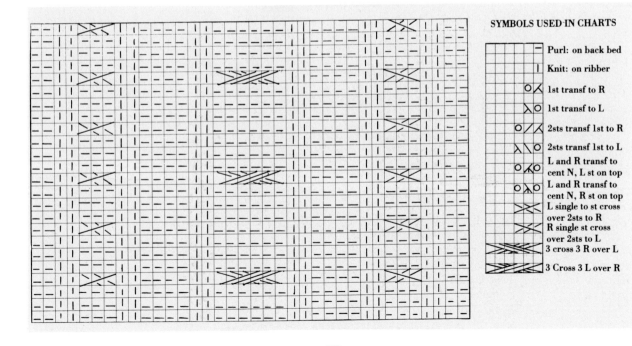

SYMBOLS USED IN CHARTS

=	Purl: on back bed
l	Knit: on ribber
O⋌	1st transf to R
⋋O	1st transf to L
O⟋⋌	2sts transf 1st to R
⋋⟍O	2sts transf 1st to L
O⋌O	L and R transf to cent N, L st on top
O⋋O	L and R transf to cent N, R st on top
⨯⋌	L single to st cross over 2sts to R
⋊⨯	R single st cross over 2sts to L
⨯⨯	3 cross 3 R over L
⨯⨯	3 Cross 3 L over R

SINGLE-BED CABLES

This sample is worked over 36Ns. Follow the cable diagram, leaving one needle at NWP either side of the cable panel where the columns of two knit stitches occur on the chart (page 33). These will emphasise the cable. The small cables were crossed every fourth row, the large ones every eighth. These rows are knitted before working the cables. The small cables are worked over three stitches: on the left the single left-hand stitch crosses two to the right, the two right-hand stitches moving one to the left. On the right this is reversed: the single right-hand stitch crosses the two to the left, whilst they move one stitch to the right

DOUBLE-BED CABLES

This is the same cable pattern as for the single bed, but the cables are emphasised by two ribber stitches at either side, arranged after working a few rows of 1×1 rib. MT8/6. Ribbed stitches give the cable a greater elasticity and more definition than the method for the single bed but, as you will see in Chapter 7 Combining Techniques, a rib stitch can be produced comparatively easily with practice, by re-forming a knit stitch instead of leaving a needle out of work (see chart page 33)

· · · · · · · · · · · · · ·

EARS OF CORN

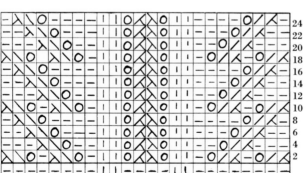

The stitch set-up is shown below the knitting chart. A 1×1 rib was worked over 40 sts, ending CAR before transferring the centre 24sts as shown, flanked by 8 sts at either side in 2×2 rib. K2r, CAR, before starting the pattern. MT8/6. The stitch transfers are then made after two knitted rows when the carriage is at the right of the machine

· · · · · · · · · ·

FAN

The sample was knitted over 50sts, allowing 2sts between each motif, on T9. This motif, adapted from a Barbara Walker chart, can be planned as an all-over design or could be combined with cables to form a panel. However, it also lends itself to a design for a collar with large scallops at the edge, and has been developed here for this purpose.

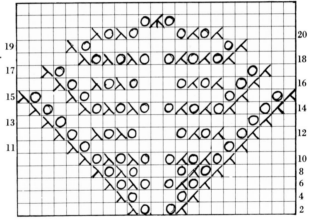

The shape of the top of the fan is worked by bringing out the non-patterning needles to holding position on each row from r16 onwards, allowing the strands of yarn to lie across the needles at HP. R24 is worked on T10, and the CO is worked behind the sinker posts, carefully incorporating the strands of yarn. The stitch transfers are made after two knitted rows, marked at the right of the chart. A number at the left means you transfer on that row also

• • • • • • • • • • • • • •

BOBBLES

The bobbles in this sample are worked by transferring 4sts on to a safety pin. The stitch at the right of this group, still in the needle on the main bed, marks the ultimate position of the bobble. With a separate strand of main or contrast colour, K the st on this needle by hand and E-wrap CO 4sts on the empty Ns (5sts). Handknit 3rs. 4th r, dec 1st each edge, twice. 1st remains on centre N. Using single transfer tool, lift a strand of yarn from each bottom corner of the CO row, and place on centre N. Transfer these to N5 at R. Push bobble through to back of work. Replace sts from safety pin on to Ns, taking care not to twist sts. Continue knitting. Several bobbles of different colours can be worked in one row. The ends are sewn in carefully afterwards

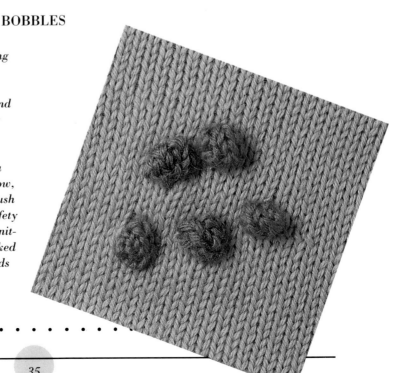

• • • • • • • • • • • • • •

6

SHORT-ROW *Patterning*

SHORT-ROW PATTERNING CAN BE CONSIDERED a hand technique insofar as the needles are manipulated at holding position to produce areas of colour but, as you will see, punchcard or mylar Fair Isle patterning can be incorporated in chosen areas. It is great fun to work, but can be frustrating if you do not remember a few rules.

If you have never used holding position for garment shaping, at the neckline in particular, you probably haven't met the term 'automatic wrapping'. Shaping or patterning in this technique without wrapping the yarn around the first needle in hold will leave a small hole in the work. This can be decorative, as in the All-in-one Raglan Sweaters (p62), but if you do not want the hole – and you would avoid this if you were shaping panels in a sideways-knitted skirt, for example – then instead of wrapping the yarn around the needle by hand, you can work as follows:

CO 40sts. K several rs ending CAR.
(This example shapes in groups of 5 stitches.)
Bring all Ns execpt for last 6 at R to HP. Set carr to HP.
K to L. Bring out last N knitted to HP. Yarn will wrap over this on next row.
K to R. Push 6Ns back from HP to UWP.
K to L. Bring out last N knitted to HP.
K to R. Push 6Ns back from HP to UWP.
Continue like this until all Ns are knitted back to WP. End with CAR.
Bring 4Ns at L of work to HP. K to L.
Bring 5th N from L to HP. K to R.
Continue until all Ns are at HP and CAR.
Set carr to K back to WP, and knit a few rows.
Stitch groups can be any number of stitches you require.

A dress, skirt or jacket which is knitted vertically needs some shaping at the hemline, however slight. Six or eight rows of graded shaping will give the slight curve necessary. If a pattern shows a sloped shoulder, this benefits from being worked in short rows instead of a cast-off gradient. Finish by casting off the stitches as one row or leave on waste yarn and join to the matching shoulder on the machine.

All knitters will agree that short-row shaping makes for neatness of finish and contributes greatly to the fluidity of a garment. Its utilitarian virtues are great, but so is its design potential when colour, pattern and texture are manipulated in this way. A few practice runs, especially with diagonal stripes, changes of direction and blocks of Fair Isle, will help you to understand the technique. Blocks of tuck or slip-stitch patterns are not possible, because their structure and tensions are incompatible. Circles, too, have their problems and are better left to intarsia.

While knitting is in progress, you may find that the last two or three stitches tighten in the needles, which have been knitted back to working position as you lengthen the knitted row. If these are not eased before knitting the next row the work will distort slightly. Putting a weight below this area can help, though too much weight can prevent these stitches from knitting, and the fault may then be found in the tension disc of the yarn-tension unit. This often occurs when using a textured yarn on the chunky machine. Yarn, machine and knitters vary; practice is very important so that these problems are resolved before you start the great work. Fortunately, practice is interesting and absorbing, providing you with a library of ideas. Remember to keep records of your notable achievements for future reference – there is nothing worse than looking at a sample and wondering how you did it.

If you are mixing different yarn types you will need to work tension squares for each one, to try to produce the correct number of stitches and rows for your pattern. This may mean that different tensions will have to be set for some of the yarns. It contradicts the normal practice of adjusting the stitches and rows of a pattern according to the measurement of the square, but should not be too much of a problem since you are unlikely to choose yarns with a dramatic variation in weight. General practice is to select the tension you want for the main yarn, working your pattern from this and using it as a guide for any other yarns used.

It is essential to draw your garment shape onto stitch-related graph paper. The number of rows and stitches will depend on your main tension square, and on the garment measurements. You do not need to search for the arithmetically correct stitch-to-row ratio; all you need is graph paper large enough for your project, which takes into account that a stitch is more nearly represented by a rectangle than a square. Mylar and punchcard papers are printed like this, but are of course too small for this purpose. With the full garment shape drawn out, sleeve, shoulder and neck shapings included, the design can be matched front to back, ignoring side seams if you want to give a continuous impression.

The simplest machine-knitted garment takes longer to plan than it does to knit. The machine is fast, and is going to reach the finishing tape long before hands and needles, but above all it is a craft tool, and few techniques better express its service to ingenuity and creativity than the manipulation of stitches in short-row shaping. While you are sampling you are improving your technique and developing your colour sense, and what you finally produce will not be expressed in hours but in the way your garment shows your sensitivity to materials, colour and form.

· · · · · · · · · · · ·

SHORT-ROW KNITTING

Short-row knitting with a gradient formed by one stitch per row – not always easy to understand when pushing needles back to working position. You climb the diagonal one row and one stitch at a time.

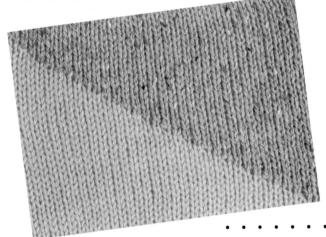

With col A cast on 40sts CAR.
K to L. Set carr to HP.
Bring N20 at L to HP, K to R.
Bring N19 at L to HP, K to L.
Bring N18 at L to HP, K to R.
Bring N17 at L to HP, K to L.
You will notice that as you knit to the right the yarn is wrapped over the last needle brought out to hold.
Continue knitting like this, shortening the rows, until all needles are at holding position. Break yarn and take the carriage over to the left.
Join in col B.
Push 3Ns to UWP, K to R.
Bring last N back to HP, K to L.
(Two needles for two rows, one for wrapping.)
Continue knitting like this, lengthening the rows, until all needles are back at working position.

· · · · · · · · · · · ·

A STEEPER GRADIENT

Short-row knitting with a gradient formed by 1 stitch every 2 rows. You climb the diagonal two rows and one stitch at a time.
With col A cast on 40sts CAR.
K to L. Set carr to HP.
Bring N20 at L to HP, K to R.
K to L.
Bring N19 at L to HP, K to R.
K to L
Continue like this until all Ns are at HP.
Break yarn and take carr over to L.
Join in yarn B.
Push 2Ns to UWP, K to R.
(One needle for two rows, one for wrapping.)
Bring last N back to HP, K to L.
Continue knitting like this until all needles are back at working position.

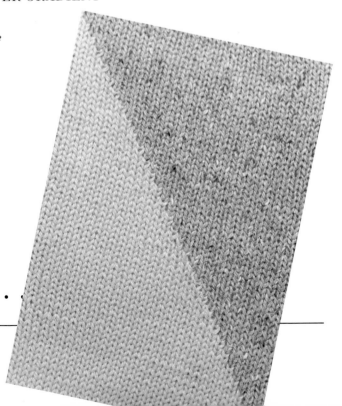

· · · · · · · ·

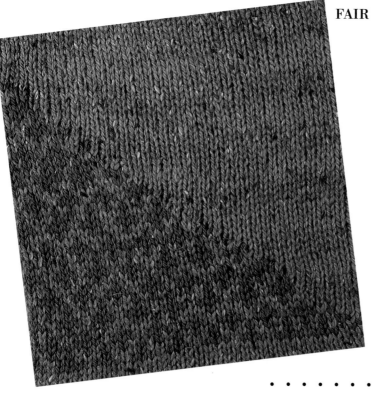

FAIR ISLE

In Fair Isle, needles at holding position knit back automatically to working position in the contrast colour (feeder B), and do not pattern. This does not matter if you are shaping one stitch at a time, but if you are shaping in groups of stitches they need to be replaced manually to working position. The pattern will not be affected as you shorten the rows, so it is quicker to work the Fair Isle if you can arrange your design to do this. The Fair Isle was knitted first in this sample, the stripes as the rows were lengthened. The shaping is one stitch per row.

Fair Isle patterning can be incorporated in this technique

• • • • • • • • • • • •

ZIG-ZAGS

This sample is worth trying if you plan to work diagonal stripes. The diagram shows you the order of working. Cast on 40sts and K1r to L, bring 30sts at R to HP. Shorten the rs at L, then change colour and put Ns 0-10 at L of centre O to UWP. Now when you knit to the left you are lengthening the rows, so you need to push back three needles to upper working position. The rows are being shortened at the right, so you will bring a needle to hold on each row. It is easy to get into a muddle at first. Check that you keep the correct number of needles working. Again, the shaping is one stitch per row.

You can practise simple gradients without a diagram, but you must draw one out if you want to knit zig-zags

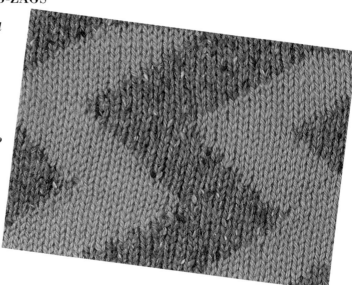

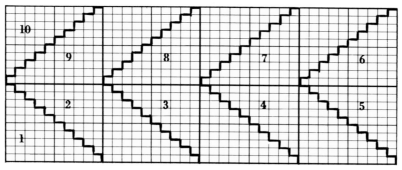

• • • • • • • • • • • •

INTERSECTING DIAGONALS

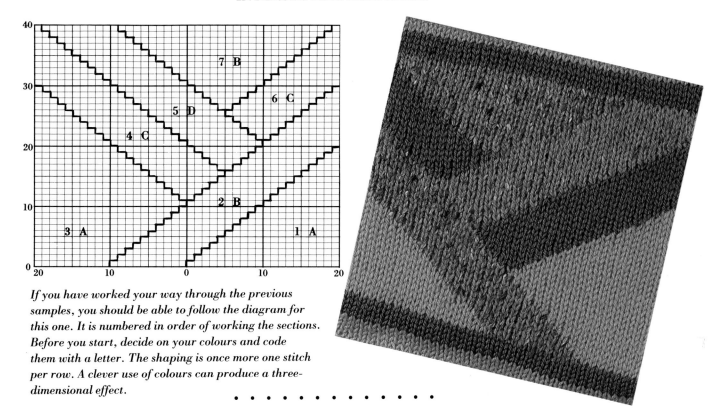

If you have worked your way through the previous samples, you should be able to follow the diagram for this one. It is numbered in order of working the sections. Before you start, decide on your colours and code them with a letter. The shaping is once more one stitch per row. A clever use of colours can produce a three-dimensional effect.

• • • • • • • • • • • •

DIAMONDS AND CURVES (Instructions p40)

Follow the order of working on the diagrams. Be careful to weight the work as necessary. Curves should first be drawn onto the graph paper, then squared off to produce a working diagram as shown. The large diamond is shaped one stitch over two rows. It is not possible to shape any steeper than this by this method; you would need to work verticals either by intarsia, or by holding the sections not being knitted, knitting those to match, and blind-stitching any vertical gap this caused. A sample of the reverse side of the knitting is shown, with the ends sewn in. The reverse often looks so satisfyingly neat that it is a shame to hide it! (See previous page, bottom.)

From this diamond you can plot how to work a triangle sitting on its apex or its base. Full written instructions are given to help you relate them to the diagrams.

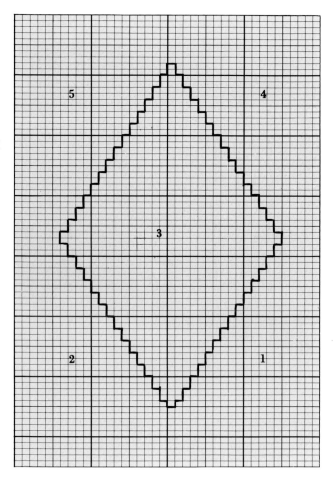

INSTRUCTIONS FOR LARGE DIAMOND

CO 40sts MY. K 20rs, ending CAR.
Set carr to HP.
Bring 20Ns to L of centre O to HP.

K section 1 first:
K to L. Bring N1 at R to HP, K to R.
K to L. Bring N2 at R to HP, K to R.
Continue like this until N15 is at HP, 5sts remain at WP, carr is at R.
Bring last 5sts at R to HP. Break yarn.

Section 2:
CAL, Push all Ns to L of centre O to UWP.
K to R. Bring N1 at L to HP, K to L.
K to R. Bring N2 at L to HP, K to L.
Finish to match section 1. All Ns are at HP.

Section 3:
In contrast yarn:
CAR, N1 to L of centre O to UWP, K to L.
N1 to R of centre O, K to R.

Repeat with Ns 2,2; 3,3; until 5sts remain at L and R, ending CAR.
Now bring N nearest the carr to HP, K to L.
Continue like this, knitting to R and L until all Ns are at HP.

Section 4:
CAR. Push 6Ns at R to UWP, K to L.
Bring last N knitted to HP, K to R.
Push 2Ns to UWP, K to L.
Repeat the last 2rs until centre O is reached, ending CAR.
Bring all Ns out to HP CAR, move carr to L.

Section 5:
Push 6Ns at L to UWP, and finish section 5 as section 4, ending CAL.
K 20rs. COff.

· · · · · ·   P   A   T   T   E   R   N   I   N   G   · · · ·

SMALL DIAMOND

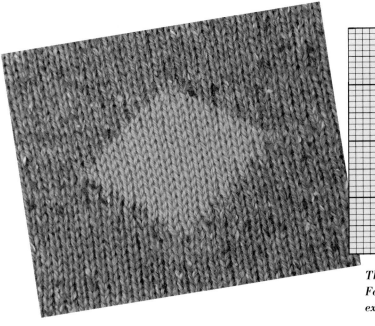

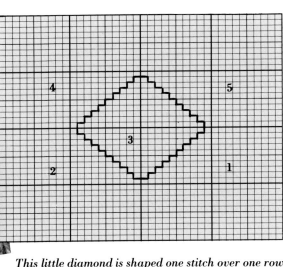

This little diamond is shaped one stitch over one row. Follow the chart; the order of shaping the sections is exactly the same as for the large diamond

• • • • • • • • • • • • • •

CURVE

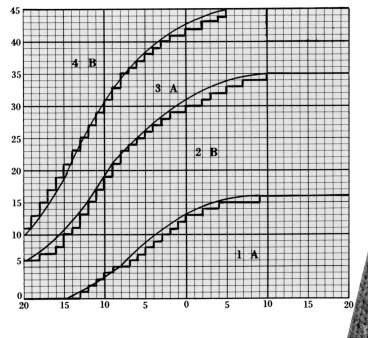

Draw curves freely on your graph paper. As you square them off for the chart you will have to make some adjustments where the gradient is too steep

• • • • • • • • • • • • • •

7

COMBINING Techniques

MACHINE AND HANDKNITTERS are inveterate collectors of knitting patterns. Whether all of these are ever used is immaterial; they form a reference library, a library which grows over the years, and can become very precious for sentimental as well as practical reasons. One of my aunts had such a collection: *Woman's Weekly* magazines dating back to the 1920s and kept solely for the knitting and crochet patterns, stacked in the spare room in neat order. Her house bore witness to their worth: knitted and crocheted chairbacks, placemats, doilies and lace curtains, cushions, a bath mat and, of course, knitted dresses, jumpers and underwear.

That collection has long since disappeared. Now my own shelves bear witness to the addiction. A survey of these patterns, and the memory of the older collection, show patterns with great versatility as well as the traditional jerseys, socks, and hat and glove sets. There were bows, collars and inserts knitted in contrast yarn and stitch. Great liberties were taken with directional knitting. Panels of cable alternated with Fair Isle or lace. These are patterns for handknitting of course, many demonstrating a freedom from the horizontal which so often dominates machine knits. Handknitting still takes imaginative leaps forward. You must remember that the machine can do almost all that a pair of needles in good hands can do, a lot more besides and faster.

To escape from the horizontal aspect of the machine, producing bands of stripes, traditional Fair Isle and modern variations, you need, at a simple level, to develop an automatic stitch pattern which has vertical or diagonal movement. You can, of course, knit the work from the side seams instead of the horizontal welts, but there are ways to combine automatic and hand techniques. The ideas here are not exhaustive, but should challenge you to develop your own. If you have not isolated areas of pattern before, refer to the instructions in your machine handbook for single-motif or single-area patterning, and knit a few samples of this first.

When mixing techniques, it is important to adapt your garment calculation if you feel that the 40st×60r tension square will not take certain stitch distortions into account. If, for example, your stitch design covers a greater area than the standard tension square and includes a variety of stitch patterns, and especially if it includes cables, it will be more sensible to measure one complete pattern area and work from that.

The samples in this chapter worked on the standard machine are all knitted in 4-ply equivalent botany wool, at tension 6. The large insert has a single end of glitter yarn added in to the second colour.

• • • • • • • • • • • •

SHORT-ROW PATTERNING WITH BOBBLE DECORATION

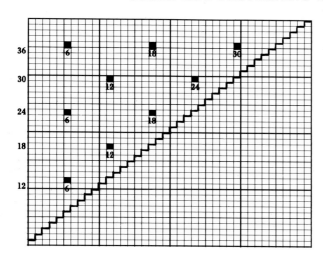

The sample was worked on a chunky machine. Instructions for the short-row shaping (one stitch per row) and the bobbles will be found in their respective chapters. The chart here shows the positioning of the bobbles, which is N5 in the instructions. The main yarns are chunky worsted-spun wool, and a luxury mohair; the bobbles are in a handknitting 70% angora 30% wool yarn. The multi-coloured knops in the mohair tend to predominate on the purl side of the knitted fabric, but are easily pushed through to the knit side.

Remember you are reading the chart from the purl side when you plan your designs, as comparison with the finished sample demonstrates

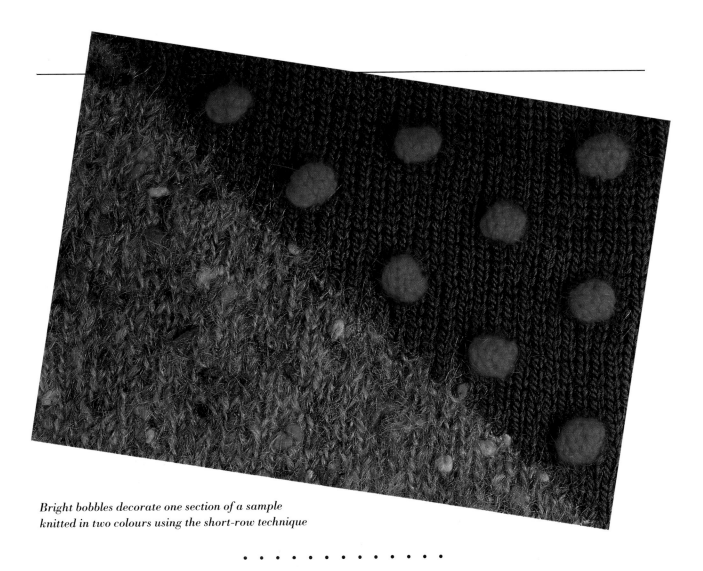

*Bright bobbles decorate one section of a sample
knitted in two colours using the short-row technique*

. . . .

EXPANDED CABLE WITH BOBBLE INFILL (MAIN BED + RIBBER)

Bobbles can nestle comfortably in an open cable, giving textural and colourful detail to a garment. These smaller bobbles, sometimes charmingly called 'popcorns' can be knitted before the main section and added in where necessary, or worked whilst knitting is in progress, as they were here.

INSTRUCTIONS: The cable is worked over 11sts in the centre of a 40st sample, and is flanked by 5sts on the ribber (see needle setting). The yarn used here is 4-ply equivalent botany wool; small ends of contrast are needed for the bobbles, and a couple of metres of main yarn to knit 4rs 11-14 on the centre 7sts by hand. Read the written instructions in conjunction with the diagram. They are easier to understand as you work the knitting, since the movement and creation of stitches is logical. If you also refer to the chart you will very soon understand what to do, as stitches travel across the work before and after the cable is crossed.

Widening the cable gives extra room for small bobbles to nestle in the centre

. . . .

CO 40sts 1×1 rib. K several rs T3/3 ending CAR.
Arrange sts as diagram, leaving sts either side as 1×1 rib.
RC000 K 6rs. CAR. Transfer as follows:
r7 *Using triple-transfer tool, move sides of cable on MB 1N towards centre. Push empty Ns to NWP. Transfer outside edge sts of cable centre on RB to MB N above (2sts on N.)
Bring to WP on RB a 6th N on inside edge of flanking sts. With double-ended bodkin, transfer heel of outside cable st to this N.
K 2rs*.
Repeat from *to* once more, bringing up 7th N at RC10.
Now with spare MY, K 4rs on the centre 7sts by hand.
Trim ends to 10cm/4in. Draw through between beds.
Make cable cross, 3st over 3st, as diagram. Ignore single ribber st in centre, but be careful not to lose it!
Bringing centre 7sts to HP each time, carr set to K, K 2rs across all sts. RC12.
r13 *Using triple-transfer tool, move sides of cable on MB 1N out from centre.
Push empty N to NWP. Transfer inside sts of flanking sts on RB to outside edge sts of cable on MB. (2sts on N.)
Bring to WP Ns either side of cable centre on RB.
Transfer heel of inside-edge cable sts from MB to RB*.
K 2rs.
Repeat from *to*.
r15 (you have just finished *to* above) also make bobble as follows:
With contrast yarn cast on by hand 3sts on MB at cable centre. CAR.
Handknit 4rs.
Pick up a strand of yarn from sts 1 and 3 of CO edge, transfer to corresponding Ns, pull through st on needle.

Now transfer sts 1 and 3 to centre N and handknit.
Transfer this st to centre N of cable centre on RB.
Trim ends to 10cm/4in and push down between beds.
Knit row.
Continue knitting, making bobbles on rs 19 and 23.
On r 24 you start moving the cable in again.
After crossing and moving out, finish sample with 6rs K.
Transfer to MB and COff.

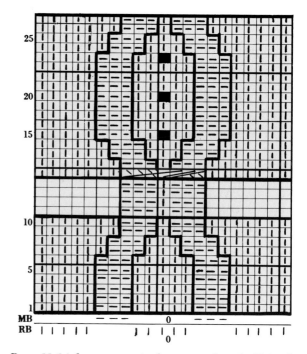

Rows 11-14 do not count in the pattern length. Knitted by hand with spare yarn, they ease the crossing of the cable

• • • • • • • • • • • •

INSERTS

These decorative two-colour squares are set on a contrasting background which can also be knitted in two colours. The techniques involved are single-bed Fair Isle and holding position, providing for greater use of colour across the knitting without using a colour changer. On a garment with several inserts, each one can be a different colour combination.
If the yarn type is contrasted as well you will need to balance the tensions. To avoid distortion the insert must measure the same as the background.
The small inserts shown here are suitable for all machines with a 24st repeat, and on these machines the position of the insert must relate to the area of the needle bed marked for this purpose. This will govern their position on a garment. If you hand select the end needles you can increase the width to 26sts, and if you are prepared to do a little extra

hand work you can increase the width even more by hand selecting pattern needles. Electronic machines give a greater freedom for insert size and placement, but success depends more on colour combinations for impact.

INSTRUCTIONS: The larger sample is worked over 72sts and 96rs using 4-ply equivalent botany wool. Two alternative small inserts are shown, one over 25sts and one over 26sts, hand selecting end needles as needed. Remember to reset your row counter each time you knit a section, and to turn it back one row after setting the pattern. The extra stitches at the edges of the insert are knitted together with the edge stitches of the pattern on the first row of the final section, and prevent a reduction in the size of the insert when sewing up. If you have end-needle selection they will knit in contrast yarn. If you do not want them to do this, push them back to WP on each row.

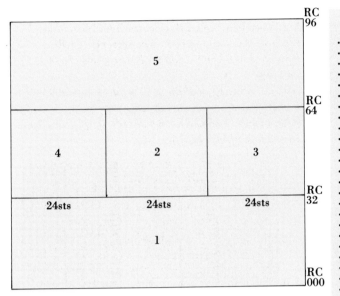

RC
96

RC
64

RC
32

RC
000

5

4   2   3

24sts   24sts   24sts

1

This diagram shows the order of knitting the sections.
Sections 1, 3, 4 and 5 are knitted in two-colour Fair
Isle technique in an all-over background pattern.
The insert section, 2, contrasts in colour and design,
achieved by holding sections 3 and 4 – not nearly as
complicated as it looks! The motif is knitted over 24sts
and 30 or 32rs. Look at cross-stitch designs and old tiles
for inspiration.

(Instructions continued on p46)

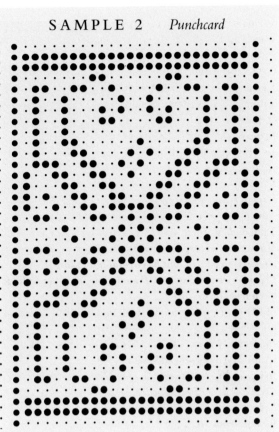

S A M P L E   2   *Punchcard*

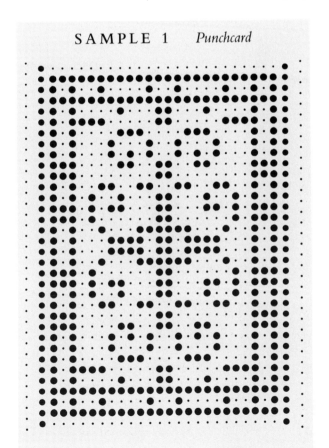

S A M P L E   1   *Punchcard*

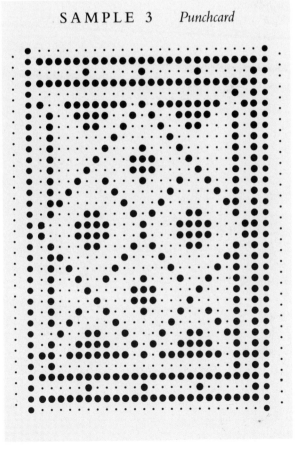

S A M P L E   3   *Punchcard*

3

1

2

4

When you have knitted section 1 in the background pattern, make a note of the last pattern row number. Break yarns.

Bringing the Ns for section 3 and 4 to HP knit the insert pattern, bringing an extra N to WP at either side (for the seam) by temporarily transferring the edge background sts to next N. Set the first row from L to R according to your machine's instructions (the carriage needs to be set to hold, slip/part/free-move for this). Knit insert. Break yarns. Replace stitch from 'borrowed' needle.

Change to background pattern and, with Ns for sections 4 and 2 at HP, replace section 3 ns to WP using transfer tool.

'Borrow' an extra N as before, and set the recorded pattern row from L to R and K to RC64. Record pattern row. Break yarns.

Now with sections 2 and 3 at HP replace section 4 Ns to WP, borrowing an extra N again. Set recorded row from R to L and K section 4 in background pattern. RC64. Break yarns.

With all Ns at WP and with 2sts on each of the 4 edge Ns, set recorded pattern row from L to R and knit to RC96. COff. You now have an insert with two vertical slits. Carefully mattress-stitch these together to give an invisible join.

SAMPLE 4 *Mylar sheet*

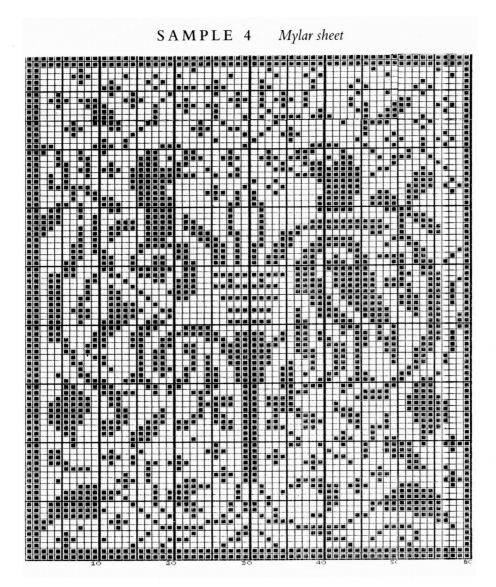

Developed from a Celtic design, this insert panel is planned for the electronic and is 60sts by 86rs. The original pattern was made for cross stitch but it is not possible to transfer it directly to a knitting chart because it is on a square grid, whereas the knitted stitch is a rectangle. It was photocopied, enlarged, and the outline traced. This was transferred to the mylar design paper, from which the final design was traced onto the transparent mylar sheet. 6rs less would have given a perfect square, but with some loss to the overall design.

N31 at the right of the panel was brought out to HP on each row. It then knits in the contrast colour, giving a 2st border to match the opposite edge. Otherwise, mark the mylar sheet at N29 at the right of each row. The method for incorporating it into a patterned background is identical to the smaller squares. The method is the same if you want a plain background, but in a colour contrasting with those of the motif. Otherwise, any of these designs can be knitted as a single motif

• • • • • • • • • • • •

FAIR ISLE AND CABLES

Many of the old patterns combined embroidery with cables – much quicker to combine automatic Fair Isle with cables and add a little Swiss darning for emphasis. It does take a little longer, but it makes the act of knitting more interesting and the end result rather special.

The samples here are designed for 24st repeats and are suitable for automatic and electronic machines. Electronic owners have a greater flexibility widthways, but the knitting hints on page 48 are the same for all machines.

SETTING UP THE NEEDLE ORDER

The Fair Isle panel knits better if it has the minimum of 1st in MY at either side. In these samples the design is 14sts wide, plus 2 edge sts in MY; 16sts in all. There are 8sts left for the cable panel. Needles 1 and 8 of this panel are pushed to NWP, leaving 6 for transfer work. It does not sound much, but there are lots of interesting cable settings you can do over 6sts besides the obvious 3 cross 3.

KNITTING A SAMPLE

Plan your repeats across the needle bed according to your machine's instructions; make a note of the needle number of the Ns at NWP. Plan your cable and write down the rows you will make the transfers on. Remember you will transfer after you have knitted that row. Cast on the full number of sts, and after knitting a few rows transfer sts 1 and 8 to an adjacent needle before starting the pattern (see above).

FLOATS

Because the Fair Isle panel is only 16sts wide, the floats of the second colour need to be latched up at the back of the work when the knitting is finished.

END-NEEDLE SELECTION

If you have needles at NWP your machine may bring the needles at either side to UWP every time you knit a row. If you want to avoid this, cancel the end-needle selection mechanism before starting to knit.

MEASURING THE TENSION

The usual tension square is not reliable here. Knit your sample over three pattern widths and at least 60rs. After the knitting has relaxed, latch up the floats and do any Swiss darning before pressing.

Now measure the width of the repeat at the centre of the swatch, and the number of rows to 10cm/4in, and use these to calculate stitch requirements.

You may find it best to plan to have Fair Isle sections at the sides of garment pieces, so that any increases can take place in the plain area. You could leave this without cables and with all 8sts at WP.

GARMENT BANDS

These techniques reduce the width of the knitting, so plan to have fewer needles for the welts than for the main knitting, otherwise the welt could be the widest part of your sweater (see Techniques).

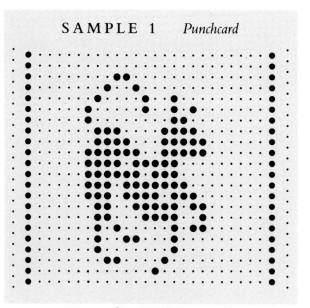

SAMPLE 1   *Punchcard*

Leaping dog

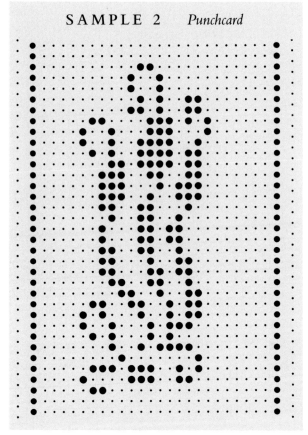

SAMPLE 2   *Punchcard*

Spring flowers

(see knitted samples, p50)

COMBINING CABLES WITH LACE

Nothing is more charming than a classic all-over lace sweater, but nothing is more interesting to knit than lace combined with cables, bobbles, Fair Isle or all three.

To prepare for an elaborate project, you need to knit samples of all the techniques you are planning to use to see if they produce the effect you want and, even more, how they affect the knitted fabric. Make notes for future reference. Plot and balance the elements of your design, and juggle with stitch groupings so that your repeats occur where you want them.

Before you start, practise cabling, re-forming stitches and, if you haven't done so before, knitting a single motif in lace according to the method for your machine. Select a lace pattern that works well over, say, 24sts and 32rs and set this in the centre of the needle bed. Then allocate the cable needles at either side, allowing at least two plain knit stitches between the two techniques.

In these samples I have re-formed a stitch at either side of the cable panel (see Techniques). In sample 1 the cable is worked over 6sts. The cable in sample 2 is also worked over 6sts but has a knit stitch at either side, making an 8st panel. This enabled me to fit cables across the work to frame the lace panel.

These samples demonstrate techniques that can be used to design sweaters with continuous vertical panels and more complex chequerboard effects, alternating the lace panels with panels of more intricate cable or bobbles, perhaps introducing colour either in stripes or Fair Isle. You cannot knit automatic Fair Isle and lace simultaneously of course, though you could always use Swiss darning on the plain stocking-stitch areas.

Mistakes are easily made when you do not have a needle out of work at either side of the cables to guide you. Mark the needle bed at either side of the cable with a soft pencil. The marks are easily erased when patterning is finished.

Don't rely on the standard tension square (see Techniques) for these designs. Measure each design unit to arrive at stitch and row numbers. Keep garment shapes simple and pay particular attention to seam lines; try to keep panels of stocking stitch at the sides of the work. Remember that the welts will need fewer stitches than the main knitting; cables and re-formed stitches reduce the width. If you use a garter carriage calculate areas of garter stitch separately, since they will measure less than the same number of rows of stocking stitch.

The sampler or patchwork effect you will achieve will be sufficient reward for your care. Practise in something economical and easy to knit with, acrylic perhaps, but knit your eventual work of art in something worthy of your efforts.

(Knitted sample 1, p50)

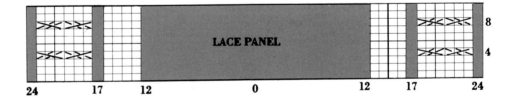

(Knitted sample 2, p50)

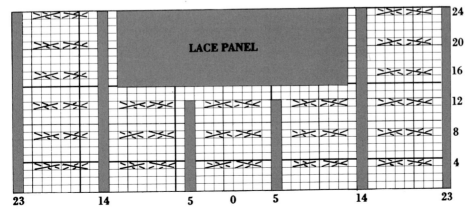

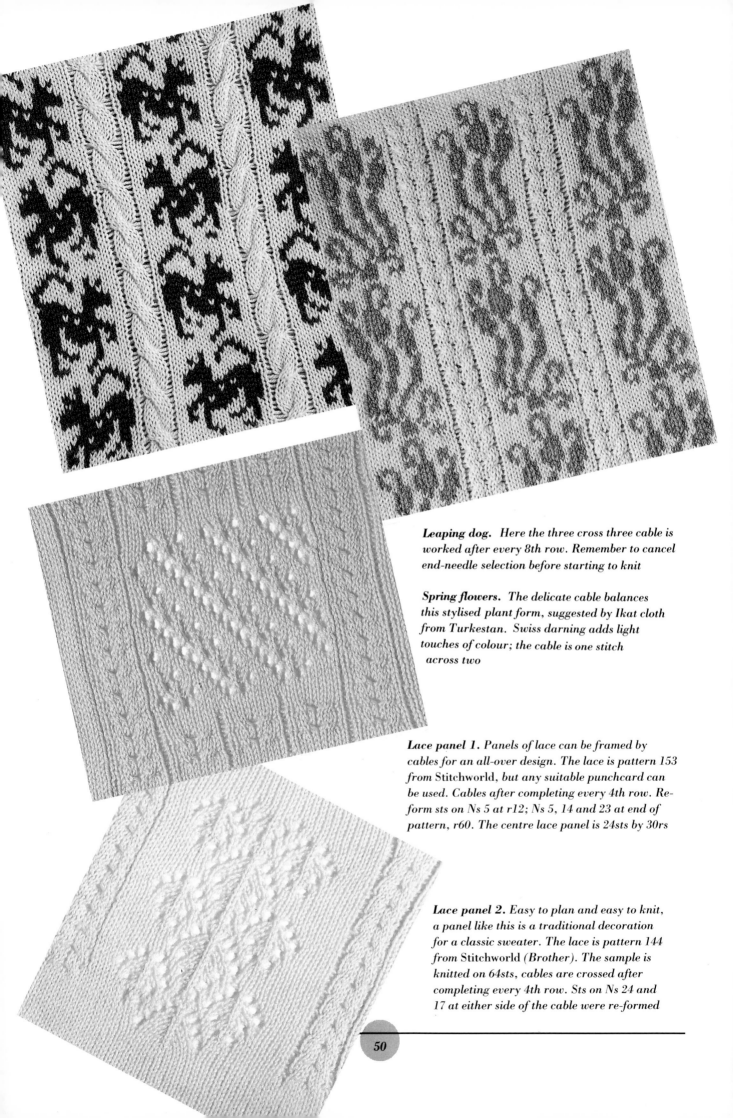

Leaping dog. Here the three cross three cable is worked after every 8th row. Remember to cancel end-needle selection before starting to knit

Spring flowers. The delicate cable balances this stylised plant form, suggested by Ikat cloth from Turkestan. Swiss darning adds light touches of colour; the cable is one stitch across two

Lace panel 1. Panels of lace can be framed by cables for an all-over design. The lace is pattern 153 from Stitchworld, but any suitable punchcard can be used. Cables after completing every 4th row. Re-form sts on Ns 5 at r12; Ns 5, 14 and 23 at end of pattern, r60. The centre lace panel is 24sts by 30rs

Lace panel 2. Easy to plan and easy to knit, a panel like this is a traditional decoration for a classic sweater. The lace is pattern 144 from Stitchworld (Brother). The sample is knitted on 64sts, cables are crossed after completing every 4th row. Sts on Ns 24 and 17 at either side of the cable were re-formed

Design
WORKSHOP

AFTER YEARS OF HANDKNITTING, occasionally daring to alter a purchased pattern but, like many handknitters, never knitting a tension square, it was not until I was taken over by the knitting machine that tension and garment construction assumed their real importance. The greater part of a machine knitter's time is spent on these fundamentals, and on stitch sampling. The machine exists for the swift realisation of ideas.

The design equipment recommended here represents an ongoing collection. Specialist and expensive items – charting device, ribber, colour changer, for example, were acquired after careful consideration, and as knitting skills and ideas expanded.

When you are new to machine knitting you may feel safer working from a given pattern, and it is certainly very satisfying when everything turns out exactly as the chosen pattern dictates. Many of the techniques explored in the previous chapters are used and developed in the patterns that follow, and demonstrate how ideas become the reality of a workable design.

As your skill and confidence grow, shapes, yarn, and stitch patterns can be altered and adapted to suit your taste, and you will have the freedom to make your own patterns. The resources in this book will help you to do this.

DESIGN EQUIPMENT

Most of us, keen amateurs and assiduous professionals alike, have favourite bits and pieces with which we surround ourselves when we settle down to work. These talismans can scarcely qualify as design equipment, but they do the job for us. My oldest and dearest tool is a penknife which belonged to my grandfather. I have been given a really efficient electric pencil sharpener, but it does not work quite the same magic as the ritual sharpening of pencils prior to working on a new design. I also have a homemade template for cut-and-sew necklines, carefully measured and cut from the ever useful cereal box, and used constantly before I discovered that there was a cheap and robust plastic one on the market. Strong and rigid to work with, it gives all sizes and shapes of necklines.

First and foremost you need a notebook in which you record details of your samplings: yarn, tension, stitch details and comments. There is nothing worse than turning up a successful sample and having to spend ages working out how it was done. You can be even more efficient and mark samples either with a reference number or a purchased swing-ticket with room to write details on it. My notebook is full of hints gleaned from other knitters, rough sketches of sweater details I have seen and colour combinations that have impressed me; a scrapbook of invaluable information. A book with squared paper aids the accuracy of quick drawings, especially if you can't draw. If you do enjoy drawing you will already have a suitable book of plain paper, maybe spiral-bound to lie flat, and perhaps watercolour crayons to bring your drawings to life.

Stitch-related graph paper is a must when designing garments in intarsia or short-row patterning, and is much less expensive than the various plastic boards sold for the purpose. Though these are wonderful to work on, the design has to be rubbed off before the board can be re-used, and is gone for ever unless recorded on graph paper for future reference. Water-based felt-tipped pens are generally provided with these boards, but for general drawing and designing, a variety of soft pencils – 3b, 4b, 5b – is useful. Their softness varies in relation to the paper you are using. They are more sympathetic to draw with than harder pencils, and encourage the nervous to make bolder and more relaxed drawing movements.

However, we all need to use a rubber from time to time, so have a soft one by your side, and also a putty rubber. These can be moulded into a point and are useful for erasing small details. You will of course need a ruler. Apart from its aid to drawing straight lines, it is more reliable than a flexible tape-measure for measuring knitting for tension purposes when it is not possible to calculate from the standard tension square, for which the special green rule for the standard machine and blue for the chunky give a high degree of accuracy. Your tape-measure will be more use to you if it has centimetres and inches marked on the same side. A French curve helps with armholes and necklines. One knitting machine manufacturer produces a very useful combination of transparent curve and rule.

A charting device relieves the knitter of everything but the simplest of calculations, and is either full or half scale in relation to the finished knitting, built in or separate from the machine according to make and model. If yours is supplied with a transparent sheet you can store favourite and frequently used patterns on dressmaker's design paper. They are then ready to be traced onto the sheet whenever needed.

If you are making a pattern diagram with all your stitch, row and shaping information written in, then a calculator is indispensable.

Depending on your machine, you will need extra blank punchcards. Even better and less wasteful, because you can cut the length you want, is a punchcard roll, and a punch for the design. Sellotape, or special punchcard tape, repairs a wrongly punched hole; remember to stick it to both sides of the card and re-punch holes inadvertently covered. (Mylar sheets and the appropriate marker are available for electronic machines.)

If you doubt the elasticity of your yarn, reels of elastic for knitting into cuffs and welts are sold in a variety of basic colours. They don't have to be an exact match but, as with sewing cotton, invisibility is improved if a tone darker than the original yarn is used. Glass-headed pins are less likely to go missing in the depths of the knitted fabric than are the standard dressmakers' pins. They are easily avoided by the iron when pressing. They are also easier to find in the garment after sewing up.

This should be done with a tapestry needle; a packet of mixed sizes should cope with most yarns, though it is best to strand thick yarns both for ease of threading and to avoid a bulky seam. Tapestry needles have rounded blunt points to avoid splitting the yarn. You will need a small pair of needlework

scissors and, if you are keen on cut-and-sew, a good pair of dressmakers' scissors which are used for nothing else but fabric.

Obviously you will acquire equipment as you need it, and you may have special items of your own not mentioned here, perhaps even an expensive linking or overlocking machine. Machine-knitting technology may find you provided with screen, mouse, keyboard, printer and software that does away with much of the humbler items, but you still provide the input of imagination and ideas, whatever gadgets you use to arrive at the knitting stage. However you set about making your own designs almost inevitably there will be moments of frustration and disappointment. These will all be forgotten when it turns out as planned, and the planning is all your own.

COLOUR AND YARN

Though we may rarely think about it, colour is a dominant factor in our lives. It is everywhere; rural and urban landscapes are coloured by seasons and weather, sunsets and sunrise. Velvety-black skies, miserable grey days, mountains, rocks, flowers and lichens can all be evaluated in terms of colour. And then there are our own personal colours: of hair, eyes and skin tone.

Most of these are uncontrived, but from the earliest civilisations man has incorporated colour in fetish, in recording ceremonies and events, as a declaration of status, in decoration of buildings, and in replicating landscape and figurative subjects on wall and canvas; and, more imaginatively, in an abstract sense to express response to visual stimuli, feelings and ideas. So colour touches everything, and in textiles, which includes machine knitting, it is colour which draws the eye first, after which we assess style, workmanship and wearability.

When choosing colours we are often faint-hearted. We play safe, having strong, ingrained personal preferences. We obstinately stick to colour choices we think best suited to our natural colouring, perhaps going slightly mad (and perhaps slightly wrong) when we need something for a special occasion. If you are neither professionally involved with colour in some way nor a gifted amateur, you may feel inadequate when it comes to choosing colour combinations for your knitting. There are some people who have natural ability in this as in everything else, but everyone has difficulties at their own level. Even those with an innate colour sense

spend a lot of time with their eyes wide open, looking at nature, at ethnic textiles, at reference books, and at other knitters' work.

If you want to learn more about colour, you must do the same. As you pore over reference books or closely examine a mossy wall, you will recognise that famous designers have been there before you in their search for inspiration.

But the transition has to be made from ideas to practical application via the shade catalogue, not always easy when the colour range may be represented by a few weedy strands of yarn. Most of us know how very different in colour the same yarn can look in hank or cone, and even different dye lots of the same catalogue colour may vary sufficiently to disappoint. Designers have a large range of their favourite yarns in a wide spectrum of colour and can wrap lengths around a card in sequence to judge how they work together, an advantage amateur enthusiasts can't often afford to imitate. The best we can do is to look at source material with colour combinations that inspire us, and match these to the shade cards. (Chapter 1 discusses the merits of the different yarns that are available.)

It is relatively easy to make decisions about contrasting colours; blending and harmonising take more care and time. Study the samples in the pattern section. You do not have to accept these; you may disagree, but do so constructively. You will also discover that pattern texture and yarn type influence colour too, so that you can knit with two different yarns of the same colour to give a subtle shadow effect. Black botany yarn used as a main colour with black chenille in the second feeder for a simple Fair Isle design with a strong motif, gives a subtle and sophisticated shadow effect.

Collect inspirational material. Some wrapping papers are really beautiful and should be collected in a folder and not thrown away when presents are unwrapped. Cut out likely source material from magazines. Museum postcards are easily collected, covering a great range of textiles and decorative artefacts, and are widely available from bookshops as well as from the museums themselves. Pottery, both contemporary and antique, wallpaper and textile designs, will all stimulate your imagination, as can paintings; many contemporary sweaters do homage to Matisse, Miró and Mondrian. Above all, look at the work of other knitters. There is no shame in following the same path. Eventually your own style will evolve.

SHAPES

Nowadays most patterns are presented visually. Shape diagrams and stitch charts with the minimum of written instructions have made knitting much simpler. Visual presentation has also de-mystified the designer's skill and made designing available to all knitters. The shape diagram is there with all the measurements written in, easily adapted for your yarn and stitch needs, and easily transferred to the charting device.

Present-day garments tend to be roomy, to say the least. The set-in sleeve is rarely seen except in nostalgic patterns. Most garments are variations on the 'T' shape, armhole and shoulder shaping being minimal or non-existent.

However, these simple shapes and voluminous garments do not suit everyone. At the other end of the scale is the close-fitting twinset which, along with a string of artificial pearls, conjures up an image of prim conformity. This is no longer deserved, since the reason for its formality lay in the context of the work place. Now anything goes, more or less, so you can wear a twinset because it suits you and you like it.

It makes sense to have a shape library at your fingertips, since you will not only want to vary the shapes of garments you will knit for yourself, but may also have others to knit for, with their special requirements.

Fundamental variations in garment shape occur at armhole and neckline. Fashion moves hemlines of dresses and skirts and waistbands of sweaters up and down, and influences sleeve shapes, collars and pockets. Creative ingenuity turns a simple body covering into a decorative feature which can demonstrate personal taste and reflect personality. It can even make a statement about social standing – reflect on the social implication of a classic cashmere sweater.

Knitting methods can also influence shapes. Traditional handknitted Icelandic or Norwegian sweaters are worked on four or five needles, or, better still, long wires – nylon these days – with a knitting pin of sufficient length to work with at either end. The sweater is knitted as a tube, in fact like a massive sock: so much easier than knitting several pieces and joining them together. The top of the sweater is knitted, shaped and distinctively patterned all in one piece. Here is economy in technique producing a traditional style. It can be imitated on the machine, combining knitting techniques that are intriguing to work, but labour-intensive in machine-knitting terms.

There are parallels in technique developed from the technology of the machine. The use of holding position for patterning and shaping is the most obvious one, but the facility to pick up along edges of knitting to join sections on the machine is one most machine knitters use for neatness and in order to reduce sewing up. Shoulders can be cast off together, sleeve stitches picked up and knitted downwards from the armhole. Garment necklines are not cast off, but shaped using holding position, so that the neckband can continue on the neckline stitches, be turned and cast off. These methods influence the armhole shape in particular. When fashion dictated the dropped shoulder and deep armhole many machine knitters heaved a sigh of relief: no more shoulder or armhole shaping. The popularity of the slash neckline also meant the new knitter was able to produce fashionable sweaters with basic technical know-how, garments requiring little further attention when finally removed from the machine.

The basic shapes shown on pages 56–58 are a guide to calculate from or to draw onto the charting device; the method for calculating rows, stitches and shaping is given too.

Many people are not familiar with the method of taking measurements, so this is dealt with first. From these a rough diagram can be drawn, inserting relevant measurements. It is awkward to measure yourself, and easy to make mistakes, so ask someone to do it for you if possible. When choosing a shape or knitting pattern for yourself, be honest; take any figure idiosyncracies into account! For example, raglan armholes are not always the best way to disguise sloping shoulders.

Before you start knitting, whether you are following a pattern to the letter, or using it as a springboard for your own ideas, *read it through carefully*. Using waste yarn, practise any technique that is new to you. Draw the shape onto the charting device, if used, or onto paper. Use square-marked paper if possible, and make your drawing large and clear. Then, if you are not using a charter, you will need to mark in the stitch and row requirements for your own measurements, calculated from your tension square, and any shaping information. You will need to do this whether you are using the yarn recommended in the pattern, or making a substitution.

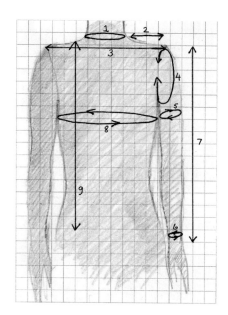

1 *Where to measure. These measurements are given as an example. They represent actual body measurements. Unless you are knitting a figure-tight garment, you will need to add about 10cm/4in tolerance (ease) on all horizontal measurements except for shoulder and neck, according to preference and style*

1 Neck, where a round neckline would occur. 36cm/14in
2 Shoulder. Neck to point. 10cm/4in
3 Front between shoulder points. 38cm/15in
4 Armhole. Measure closely round from shoulder point. 36cm/14in
5 Upper arm at fullest part. 28cm/11in
6 Wrist at narrowest part. 18cm/7in
7 Arm length, shoulder point to wrist. 53.5cm/21in
8 Bust or chest at fullest part. 97cm/38in
9 Total length according to style. Up to 66cm/26in

2 *These are the measurements of a casual sweater to fit the body measurements above*

1 Neck. 41cm/16in
2 Shoulder. 15cm/6in
3 Front. 50.5cm/20in
4 Armhole. 50.5cm/20in
5 —
6 Wrist. 26cm/10in
7 Arm. 48cm/19in
8 Bust or chest. 118cm/46in
9 Length. 66cm/26in
10 The depth of a 'V' neck depends on personal choice

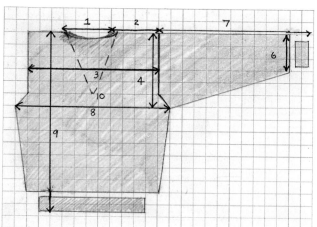

3 *The simplest shape of all. Only the sleeves have graded shaping. (Inset): Suggested plain round neckline with a tab front*

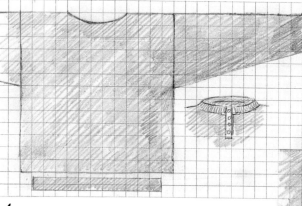

4 *Differing from shape 3 at the armhole, here approximately 5cm/2in of sts are cast off. The bodice is gently shaped from waistline to underarm as in shape 2 and 5cm/2in of sts are cast off at the armhole. This alters shoulder width and sleeve length. 5cm/2in of rows at the top of the sleeve is knitted straight to fit the armhole. (Inset): Straight ribbed collar with a tab front*

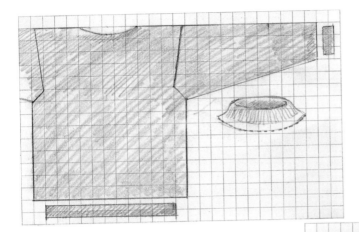

5 Very similar to shape 2, but after shaping at the underarm the armhole edge is increased for a larger drop in the shoulder. Only 3 or 4 sts are needed, suitably spaced to give a good line. This alters shoulder width and sleeve length slightly, but not the shape of the sleeve head, though the diagram suggests otherwise. (Inset): Crew neck. Details for all these necklines appear in the patterns, and they are interchangeable, as are all the details on these shapes

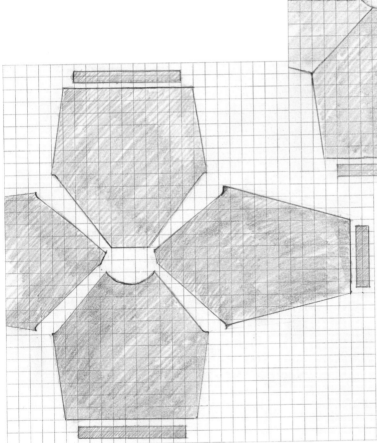

6 Basic classic raglan. A comfortable style with a deep armhole. You can make fully fashioned shapings, giving a good finish to the armhole seam, or knit the shaping using holding position. This technique is given in the patterns

7 Garment sections of the raglan, showing how each piece is shaped at the neckline

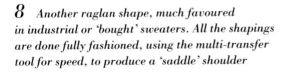

8 Another raglan shape, much favoured in industrial or 'bought' sweaters. All the shapings are done fully fashioned, using the multi-transfer tool for speed, to produce a 'saddle' shoulder

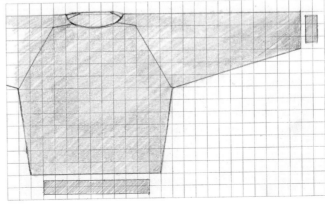

9 *Garment sections showing how the pieces in design 8 are shaped at shoulder and neckline*

10 *Back to the basic shape, but with a saddle shoulder. The garment back is the same as the front, but with no neck shaping. Short-row shaping as you knit the neckband gives the back neck height. An ideal style for a sweater in fisherman's rib*

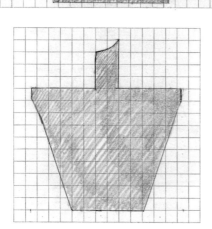

11 *The sleeve, showing the saddle shoulder of design 10*

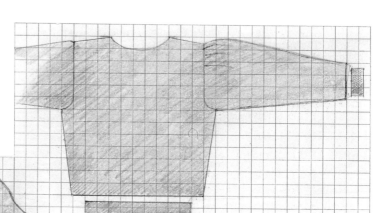

12 *Sweater with a set-in sleeve. The shoulders have graded shaping. The sleeve needs to be slightly gathered to fit the armhole*

13 *The shaping of the 'puffed' sleeve head is explained in the pattern section. A short sleeve in this style is perfect knitted in a summer-weight cotton*

CALCULATING ROWS, STITCHES AND SHAPING

The following is a step-by-step guide to calculating rows, stitches and shaping for a sweater from the measurements of a tension square.

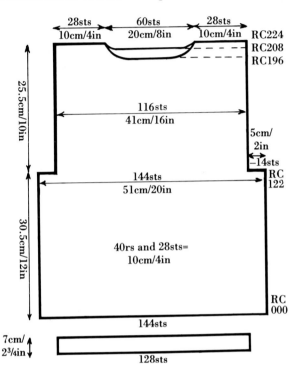

Make a clear, simple diagram. The one above will serve as an example, large enough to enter all the necessary measurements, rows, stitches and shaping information. The measurements are given in centimetres, with the approximate equivalent in inches. Work in whichever system, metric or imperial, suits you best. I have done all my calculations for this imaginary sweater using the metric system.

Measure your prepared tension square (see Techniques), and write the measurements at the top of your diagram sheet. For this example I am assuming a tension square measurement of 40rs and 28sts to a 10cm/4in square.

Calculate the rows. For easy reading while knitting from the diagram, these can be entered in red.

The length of the sweater is 56cm/22in. If you divide the row reading (40rs = 10cm/4in) by 10 to give the number of rows per centimetre (4), and multiply this by 56, this will give you the number of rows from waist to shoulder: 224. If you divide the row reading by 4 and multiply the answer by 22, you will have calculated the length from the inch reading of your tension square: 220 (equivalents are approximate). Write this on your diagram.

You now need to know when to cast off for the underarm. The length from waist to underarm is 30.5cm/12in. Your calculation will look like this:

40rs ÷ 10, ×30.5 = 4×30.5 = 122.

Write this on your diagram.

Now, in the same way work out the number of rows you need for the sleeve. The sleeve length is 48cm/20in, so the calculation looks like this:

40rs ÷ 10, ×48 = 4×48 = 192

Write this on your diagram.

Calculate the stitches. The garment width is 51cm/20in. Divide the stitch reading by 10, to give the number of stitches per centimetre, and multiply by the measurement required:

28 ÷ 10, ×51 = 2.8×51 = 142.8

Round up this decimal answer to the nearest round number: 144.

Write this on your diagram.

5cm/2in is cast off at each underarm: 14sts at each side, leaving 116sts (144 − 28).

The shoulders are 10cm/4in wide: 28sts.

This leaves 116 − 56 (two sets of shoulder stitches) for the neck: 60sts.

Calculate the neck shaping. The neckline can be drawn larger so that the detailed information is easier to see.

You have already calculated the number of stitches required for the neck. The depth in rows is calculated as before:

Front: 40rs ÷ 10, ×7 (depth of neck in cm) = 28rs
Back: 40rs ÷ 10, ×4 = 16rs

Now you need to calculate the shaping to give the curve of the neck.

Front:

You have to dispose of half the neck width at each side. Working the right side first, you need to decrease 30sts over 28rs.

Start with a straight 10cm/4in line centred at O (the garment position on the machine). The shaping can be broken down like this:

Decrease once, 14sts every 2rs. 16sts and 26rs remain.
Decrease once, 4sts every 2rs. 12sts and 24rs remain.
Decrease 12 times. 1st every 2rs.

RC224. Right front neck shaping is complete and 28 shoulder sts remain.

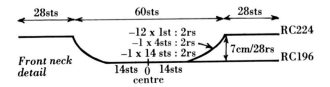

Back:

You have to dispose of 30sts over 16rs.

Start with a straight 15cm/6in line centred at O. The shaping can be broken down like this:

Decrease once, 21sts every 2rs. 9sts and 14rs remain.

Decrease twice, 2sts every 2rs. 7sts and 12rs remain.

Decrease 5 times, 1st every 2rs.

RC224. Back neck shaping is complete and 28 shoulder sts remain.

The calculations are not always achieved so easily, and stitch adjustments can be made at the centre front and back if the stitch/row allocation gives problems.

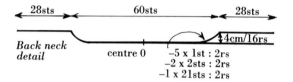

Back neck detail

28sts | 60sts | 28sts

centre 0
−5 x 1st : 2rs
−2 x 2sts : 2rs
−1 x 21sts : 2rs
4cm/16rs

Calculating the sleeves. The stitch requirements for the cuff and the armhole of the sleeve are calculated as before. The sleeves are shaped for the first 43cm/17in, the last 5cm/2in being knitted straight to fit the 5cm/2in cast off at the body underarm. So you have 192rs in which to increase from 76sts to 144sts. This means 34 increases at each armhole edge (144 − 76 = 68. 68 ÷ 2 = 34).

Divide 192 by 34 to find out how often to make the increase: 192 ÷ 34 = 5, remainder 22. So the increases will be made at both ends of every 5th row, 34 times (RC170). The last 22rs will be knitted straight.

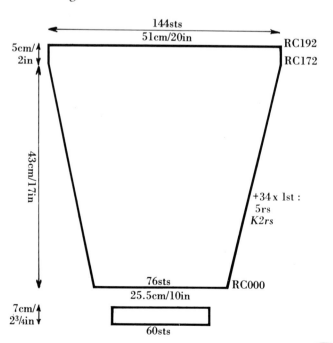

144sts
51cm/20in
RC192
RC172
5cm/2in
43cm/17in
+34 x 1st : 5rs
K2rs
76sts
RC000
25.5cm/10in
7cm/2¾in
60sts

This can be written by the side of the sleeve on your diagram:

+ 34 × 1 : 5rs, which means: increase 1st, 34 times, every 5rs.

This is done at both sides of the sleeve, of course.

Calculate the ribs. Ribbed welts are more satisfactory if they are worked on less stitches than the main knitting. Methods of increasing from welt to main knitting are given in Techniques. You will need to knit a small sample to calculate the number of rows required on the tension you prefer to give 7cm/2¾in.

Decide on the neckband. If the neck is shaped using holding position (preferable to casting off the decreases), it is easily finished in rib. This is shown in the Simple Shapes, Small Repeats patterns. Otherwise, a small stocking-stitch hem can be knitted on a finer or graded tension, working the number of rows required from a small sample.

If you want a 'V'-shaped neckline, calculate the decreases from the number of rows from the point of the 'V' to the inside edge of the shoulder.

This design is an example only, to show you how the stitches, rows and shapings are calculated, and to help you understand how to make any adjustments or alterations to the patterns in this book.

GARMENT BANDS

Front bands of a jacket or cardigan can be picked up from the edge of the knitting, and a stocking stitch hem of adequate width knitted. Approximately 2sts out of every three rows of the vertical edge will give the correct width over stocking-stitch patterns. If the edge of the knitting is not easily measured in rows, as in tuck or slip patterns, it is better to knit a sample hem over about 40sts, calculating from this the number of stitches required for the length.

For a rib band knitted separately and attached to the vertical edge, a sample will need to be knitted and measured, slightly stretched, before calculating the number of stitches to be cast on. This will avoid having too many stitches, which results in front bands that eventually stretch themselves longer than the garment itself. Vertically knitted rib bands, knitted separately and sewn to the front edge, are easily calculated from a sample knitted over the chosen stitch width for, say, 40rs. Buttonhole positions can be worked out from these samples, too.

Care is needed when measuring 'V' necks for plain hems or ribbed bands. The decreased edge of the 'V' sometimes stretches. You will need to pin out the garment to size and measure the slope. With the charting device there is no need for this; you can go straight into sampling and working out the stitch requirements as for the garment fronts above.

THE CURVED ARMHOLE AND SET-IN SLEEVE

A glance at any book on pattern drafting can be intimidating for most of us, looking as it does for all the world like a geometry text book. The relationship is far from casual; rulers, compasses and dividers are needed to produce the basic blocks these books teach us to make.

Fortunately, knitting is not a woven fabric, with little stretch either way, but a jersey mesh with flexibility width and lengthways. Working out shaping does not need to be too complex, because the knitted fabric is sympathetic to the shape of the body.

Again, as elsewhere in this book, I pay homage to Mary Weaver, whose well-thumbed books have simplified so many knitting problems. Her method of shaping the knitting for armhole and sleeve is simple and logical, and is the basis of my own. The example that follows gives a set-in sleeve to the imaginary sweater already calculated. The tension square is deemed to measure 40rs×28sts over a 10cm/4in square as before.

Instead of casting off 14sts all at once, this number is reduced over several rows to give a gradual curve. The curve will be approximately ⅓ of the total armhole length – 8cms/3in = 32rs. Then this area is itself divided into three shaping steps: an initial cast off, a gentle curve, and a steep curve.

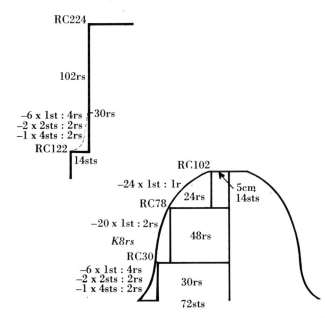

The first 'step' is 2rs only, and is an initial large step. In this case it can be 4sts.

The next can be two or three smaller steps. Here it is convenient to knit 4rs, casting off 2sts at the armhole edge, twice. This leaves 6sts to 'lose' over the remaining 26rs. Since this cannot be divided exactly, and knitting is flexible, 1st can be decreased at the armhole edge on every 4th row, 6 times in all. The decreasing in this section now finishes at row 30. The rest of the armhole is knitted straight to the shoulder.

The sleeve must now be calculated to fit this shape.

The first 30 rows of shaping can match the underarm; 10–14cm/4–5½in at the top of the sleeve will be cast off straight. (Here I have shown 28sts.)

The 28sts from both areas total 56sts, leaving 88sts to decrease on the rest of the sleeve curve (144 – 56), that is 44sts at each side between rows 30 and 102 (72rs).

This remaining area can be divided into a gentle curve, using up ⅔ of the remaining rows (48), and a steep one using ⅓ of the remaining rows (24). Decreasing on each row of the steep curve will leave 20sts to be decreased in the gently curved section of 48rs. So the easiest thing to do is to knit 8rs straight, and then decrease on every other row 20 times.

The method of writing these instructions in a simplified form is shown on the diagrams. If you look at the sleeve diagram, starting from the underarm, the shapings would read:

Decrease once, 4sts: every 2rs.
Decrease twice, 2sts: every 2rs.
Decrease 6 times, 1st: every 4rs.
Knit 8rs straight.
Decrease 20 times, 1st: every 2rs.
Decrease 24 times, 1st: every r.

The abbreviations of these instructions can be confusing at first. In the pattern diagrams they are generally written more fully, and are also detailed in the written pattern. Remember that these calculations are an example of method only, and are not a knitting pattern themselves.

Of course, all this is unnecessary if you have a charting device. You simply draw your shape according to the scale of your particular charter and knit from that, following the drawn line, increasing or decreasing according to the position on the scale. No maths required however simple!

ALL-IN-ONE RAGLAN SWEATERS

IF YOU HAVEN'T TRIED RAGLAN KNITTING in this 'all-in-one' technique you should find it fun to knit. The method was originally published in a magazine. Although no garment pattern was given, it was recommended for childrens' wear, and a sample of the technique was described. When this had been tried, an adult's sweater was worked out on the same principal. The style was comfortable and sporty and there was no reason for it to remain exclusively junior!

The original idea had one fault; there was no neck shaping indicated, back and front were the same. So, with considerable effort, I worked out short-row shaping, which was very fiddly since I was already shaping the armholes in this technique. It was easy to see why the original sample had none. Then it occurred to me to work the shaping in the neckband. Such an easy solution surely cannot be original.

The plain sweater given here is the basic design. Having knitted several garments in this technique, it became obvious that something more interesting and decorative could be done at the armhole seam. This meant altering the knitting scheme in order to knit an insert, the obvious insert being a cable pattern. I had made a couple of sweaters with cable inserts when I met an American knitter wearing a cotton tunic. Made from four straight sections of knitting, with straight sleeves, each section was joined by an insert of an intriguing design which she called 'ripple'. She demonstrated the technique, and I immediately saw its potential as a quickly worked insert for a raglan, giving the surface interest of a cable without the hard labour.

Standard Machine

Why 'All-in-One'? Instead of casting off at the armholes, and then decreasing with a transfer tool, the armhole shaping of this sweater is worked using holding position. One needle is brought to holding position on each row: at the end nearest to the carriage if you do not want a little hole in the work, at the end opposite to the carriage if you do. Each armhole and the neckline stitches are then left on waste yarn. The sleeves are begun at the top, and worked by picking up the corresponding stitches from the back and front sections from waste yarn. Neck shaping is worked in the neck band. This is a simple style easily made more special by the addition of a collar. Two antique finds are shown here

• • • • • • • • • • • • • •

Standard Machine

YARN

Celandine Sara, for machine knitting; 70% acrylic, 20% wool, 10% alpaca.
350gm/12oz = 2450m/2654yd.
1×350gm/12oz cone.
Sweater uses 200gm/7oz.

MACHINE

Standard with ribber.

TENSION

MT6, giving 28sts and 42rs to a 10cm/4in square.

MEASUREMENTS

A loose-fitting sweater. Length: 64cm/25in; chest: 112cm/44in; sleeve length: 58cm/23in from natural shoulder, 64cm/25in from neckband.

BACK and FRONT (both alike)

Welt: CO 130sts. Work 40rs 2×1 rib, T1×1, ending CAR. Transfer ribber sts to MB, K1r MT, CAL. Do not break yarn, but remove from feeder. K several rs WY and strip from machine.
Push up to WP 5 extra Ns at either side (140Ns). Re-hang work, increasing evenly across sts (see Techniques). K to R. Set RC to 002.
Inc both ends every 18th r 7 times. 154sts. RC126. CAR. Re-set RC to 000.
Shape raglan armholes: Set carr to H. On next 2rs push 6Ns to HP at opposite end to carriage.
Bringing the N at opposite end of machine to carriage to HP on every r, K to RC98 (46sts rem at WP). Break yarn. Bring all Ns to HP. Push 48Ns at R to UWP (raglan armhole sts).
K several rs in WY, strip from machine. Repeat for the 46 neck sts and for the 48sts at L.

SLEEVES

These are knitted from the top downwards and are joined to the back and front at the same time.

CO in WY 32st. K several rs, ending CAR. With wrong side of back and front sections facing, and starting with the 1st st at the neck edge, with a transfer tool replace one set of armhole sts on the needles to the L, and the other to the R, bringing the Ns to HP as you do this. Include the 6 underarm sts. The centre 32Ns remain at WP. 140Ns altogether.
Join in MY. Starting the knitting on the centre 32sts, CAR, push the N at opposite end to the carriage to UWP on every r (so that it knits back to WP). K to RC96. Now push the 6 underarm sts to UWP on the next 2rs. RC98. 140sts.

UNDERARM SHAPING

RC000. Decrease 2sts FF (use the 3 ended transfer tool, and move 3sts, 2 stitches in) at both ends of 6th and every following 8th r, 16 times altogether. RC126. K1r T8. 76sts. Break MY and leave on WY.

CUFFS

CO 68sts 2×1 rib. K39rs T1/1, 1r T3/3.
Transfer ribber sts to back bed.
With wrong side of sleeve facing, join to rib: transfer sts of last row of sleeve to Ns, decreasing evenly across the work (see Techniques). K1r T10 and COff with the latch tool.

FRONT NECKBAND

CO 80sts 2×1 rib. K 20rs T1×1. Transfer ribber sts to back bed. K 1r T6.
With wrong side of garment facing, and starting at N39 at the L, pick up 16sts from one half of sleeve top, 46 from top of one body section, 16sts from top of second sleeve and 1 extra at either end of the neckband for making up – 80sts altogether.
K 1r T10 and COff loosely, either behind the sinkers or by 'split stitch' method (see Techniques).

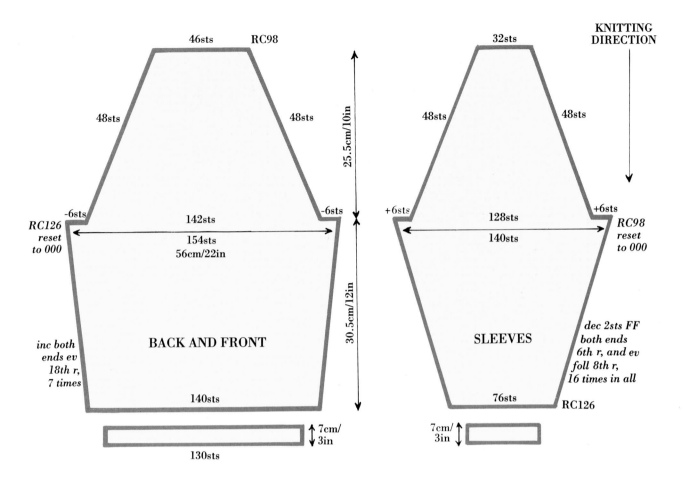

BACK AND FRONT

46sts   RC98

48sts   48sts

RC126
reset
to 000

-6sts   -6sts

142sts

154sts
56cm/22in

inc both
ends ev
18th r,
7 times

140sts

25.5cm/10in

30.5cm/12in

7cm/
3in

130sts

KNITTING
DIRECTION

32sts

48sts   48sts

+6sts   +6sts

128sts

140sts

RC98
reset
to 000

SLEEVES

dec 2sts FF
both ends
6th r, and ev
foll 8th r,
16 times in all

76sts

RC126

7cm/
3in

BACK NECKBAND

CO 80sts 2×1 rib. K 16rs. CAR.

Shape as follows: Set both carriages to H. Bring
14Ns at L to HP on both beds (28Ns altogether).
K to L. Bring last N knitted to HP, and at the same
time bring 28Ns, at R to HP on both beds. K to
R. Bring last N knitted to HP, push 11Ns at L to
UWP.

K to L.

Bring last N knitted to HP, push 11Ns at R to
UWP, K to R.

Continue shaping in groups of 10sts (N11 is for

wrapping to avoid a hole when carriage returns)
until all Ns are at WP and carr is at R. Transfer
ribber sts to back bed, K 1r T6.

Attach to garment neckline as for front neckband.

MAKING UP

Press garment with a cool, dry iron. Mattress-stitch
all rib seams, backstitch underarm and body seams.
Press seams. Fold neckband to the inside and
catch-stitch to the neck seam.

*Back of sweater showing
reversed stocking stitch
neck detail*

Chunky Tweed

*Like the sweater for the
standard machine, the armhole
shaping is worked using
holding position. However, the
sleeves are not knitted
downwards, but in the usual
way, from the cuff. Armhole
sections are then joined whilst
knitting the cable insert.
As long as you organise the
garment pieces as described in
the pattern, the technique is
quite straightforward and very
rewarding to work. The
armhole stitches waiting to be
picked up can be hung on the
sinker hooks and moved in
as necessary.
The machine will pass over
them easily*

. . . .

Chunky Designer Cotton

Originally designed as a sort of poor man's cable because it is so much quicker to work, giving a similar quality of texture and relief to the knitting, the armhole insert for this sweater achieves its sculptural quality from a clever use of holding position. Since the 'ripple' band is also used at the neck, the style is ideally suited to a machine without a ribber. The mock rib suggested in instruction books, or a plain hem would be too bulky in this thick cotton when using a single bed. It would be better to work a rib of re-formed stitches. The finished edges at the neck are allowed to roll to avoid a thick hem, and also to keep in character with the 'ripple'

Chunky Tweed

Various cable patterns were tried to give variety and interest at the raglan armhole. The traditional two cross two was easily the favourite, because it gives a higher definition to the knitted fabric. The samples are knitted in wool, which has greater stretching ability. It is possible in cotton, though you might find it easier to handknit the cable row – not too much of an imposition when the insert only involves twelve stitches. Combining the insert with the garment pieces means reorganising the all-in-one method, though the armholes are still joined on the machine

YARN

Yorkshire Mohair Mills Designer Tweed, 97% wool, 3% cotton. 50gm/2oz = 50m/55yd. 2×500gm/17oz cones.
Sweater uses 710gm/25oz.

MACHINE

Chunky with ribber.

TENSION

MT4, giving 18sts and 25rs to a 10cm/4in square.

MEASUREMENTS

A loose-fitting sweater. Length: 64cm/25in; chest: 112cm/44in; sleeve length: 58cm/23in from natural shoulder, 64cm/25in from edge of neckband.

BACK and FRONT (both alike)

Welt: CO 82sts. Work 20rs 1×1 rib, T2/2, knitting last r T3/3.
Transfer ribber sts to MB. K1r T4 CAL. Do not break yarn, but remove from feeder.
With WY in feeder, K several rs. Break yarn and strip work from machine.
Push 4 extra Ns to WP at either end (90Ns), and re-hang work, increasing evenly across sts (see Techniques). K to R. Set RC at 002.
Inc both ends every 14th r 5 times. K 6rs. RC76.
Set carr to H, reset RC to 000.
Shape raglan armholes:
Bringing the N at opposite end of machine to carriage to HP on every r, K to RC62 (38sts rem at WP). Weight the work as you knit.
Break yarn. Bring all Ns to HP. Push 31Ns at R to UWP (armhole sts). K several rs WY, working last r on T10. COff with latch tool. (It is important to COff the WY to prevent it unravelling later on).
Push 38sts at centre to UWP (neck sts) and finish on WY as before.
Push rem 31sts at L to UWP, again finishing on WY.

SLEEVES

Welt: CO 40sts. K as for back and front, increasing to 46sts and setting RC to 002 as before.
Inc both ends of every 4th r 18 times, K4rs straight. RC76. Set Carr to H, RC to 000.
Shape armholes as for back to RC62 (20sts rem at WP).
Leave sts on WY as for back.

CABLE INSERTS

1st Insert:
With ribber in position, CO 12sts in 1×1 rib. Use edge weights instead of CO comb. Work the three

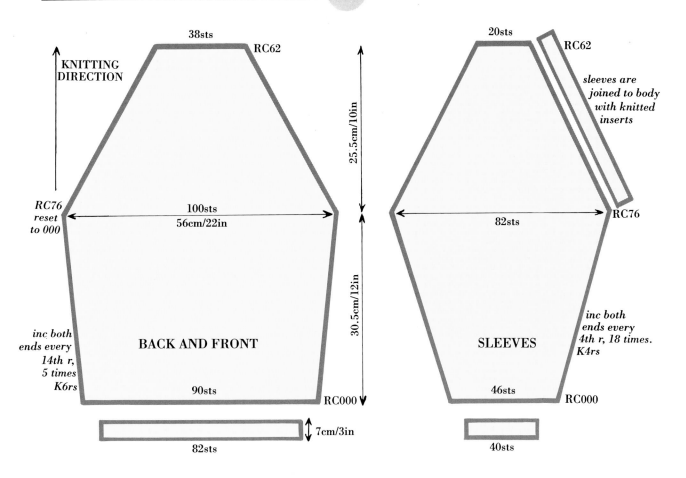

KNITTING
DIRECTION

38sts

RC62

RC76
reset
to 000

100sts
56cm/22in

25.5cm/10in

30.5cm/12in

inc both
ends every
14th r,
5 times
K6rs

BACK AND FRONT

90sts

RC000

7cm/3in

82sts

20sts

RC62

*sleeves are
joined to body
with knitted
inserts*

82sts

RC76

inc both
ends every
4th r, 18 times.
K4rs

SLEEVES

46sts

RC000

40sts

circular rs for selvedge, ending CAR. Arrange sts
for cable so that 4 centre sts are on MB, as are sts 4
and 6 at either side. 3 and 5 are on RB.
Now take one body section, wrong side facing.
Bring it up between the beds★, and put the 1st st on
WY at the L underarm onto the 1st N of insert at R.
Take one sleeve, wrong side facing, and in the
same way put the 1st st on WY at R underarm
onto the 1st N at L of insert. (2sts on end Ns).
To make the work easier to manage as you knit the
insert, push up the opposite ends of the garment
pieces between the beds and catch onto the sinker
hooks of MB. The carriage will pass over them and
they can be moved in as you knit.
RC000, T 3/3. K 2rs, CAR. With the work hook
from the ribber accessories, pick up the next armhole
st on WY between the beds and put onto the end
needles as before. Continue in this manner, picking
up the armhole sts after each even row, and at the
same time making a 2×2 cable cross R over L after
every 4th r to RC 62, when all armhole sts will be
knitted up. (NOTE: If you bring the needles out to
HP after cabling, following row is easier to knit.)
Transfer to MB, break yarn, and leave on WY,
COff as before.

2nd Insert:
Work as for 1st insert to ★.
Hang the 1st st on WY at the R underarm of the
body section on the L end needle of insert, and the
1st st of the L underarm of the 2nd sleeve on the R
end needle. K insert, crossing cables L over R.

3rd Insert:
Work as for 1st insert to ★.
Hang the 1st st at the R underarm of the sleeve on
the L end needle; the 1st st at the left underarm of
2nd body section on R end needle. K as before,
crossing cables R over L.

4th Insert:
Work as for 1st insert to ★.
Hang the 1st st at the R underarm of body on the
L end needle, and the 1st st of the L underarm of
the 1st sleeve on R end needle. Knit as before,
crossing cables L over R.

N E C K B A N D (knitted in two sections)
Front neck: CO 46sts in 1×1 rib. Work 20rs,
increasing and altering tension as follows:
Inc both ends of 2nd and every following alternate
r; rs 1-6, TO··/O··; rs7-12, T1/1; rs13-18,
T1··/1··; rs19, 20, T2/2.

Transfer ribber sts to MB★.

K 2rs T3, 1r T6. CAL.

Pick up one body section, wrong side facing, from WY at neckline, decreasing evenly by putting 2sts on a N as necessary:

7sts from top of sleeve (decreasing 3).

10sts from cable insert (decreasing 2).

32sts from front (decreasing 6).

10sts from cable insert (decreasing 2).

7sts from top of sleeve (decreasing 3).

K 1r T10 across all sts (66sts). COff with the latch tool.

Back neck: Work as for front to ★. CAR.

(NOTE: The back neck shaping is worked in ss, which will show in reverse on K side of garment.)

Set carr to H, shape back neck as follows:

Bring Ns9–33 at L of O to HP, K to L.

Bring N8 at L to HP, Ns9–33 at R to HP. K to R.

Push 8Ns at L of O to UWP. K to L.

Bring N15 at L to HP, push 8Ns to UWP at R, K to R.

Bring N15 at R to HP, push 8Ns to UWP at L, K to L.

Bring N22 at L to HP, push 8Ns to UWP at R, K to R.

Bring N22 at R to HP, push 8Ns to UWP at L, K to L.

Bring N29 at L to HP, push 8Ns to UWP at R, K to R.

Bring N29 at R to HP, push last 5Ns to UWP at L, K to L.

Push last 5Ns at R to UWP, K to R. K 1r T6.

Attach second body section, wrong side facing and finish as for front neck.

MAKING UP

Finish off ends using the latch tool; the yarn is too thick to sew in easily. Damp press, omitting ribs. Using 2 strands of MY, mattress-stitch rib seams, backstitch underarm seams. Press seams. Steam the ribs lightly by holding the hot iron above the fabric without pressing.

• • • • • • • • • • • • • • •

Chunky Cotton

●●●●●●●●●●●●●●●●●●●●●●●

1 It was not difficult to imagine this 'ripple' design as a substitute for the more labour-intensive cable. It also develops a curve at the cast-off edge which suggests the curve of a neckline. The sample in yellow cotton is knitted on a standard machine, and has a single end of gold lurex added. Not only does this add interest, but the added thickness, though minimal, gives a higher relief quality to the knitting. It doesn't have to be gold, but could be an extra end of matching cotton of approximately 2/30s thickness. If gold was added it might be more subtle to reserve it for the inserts only. The magenta sample is worked on the chunky machine. In the resulting pattern the armholes are still joined on the machine, but in yet another method from the other two designs

❶

YARN
Yorkshire Mohair Mills Designer Cotton DK; 100% cotton. 50gm/2oz = 85m/95yd. 2×500gm/17oz cones. Sweater uses 740gms/26oz.

MACHINE
Chunky with ribber.

TENSION
MT3, giving 18sts and 25rs to a 10cm/4in square.

MEASUREMENTS
As for sweater in Designer Tweed. Use the same diagram. It is recommended you make up the finished garment with a matching sewing cotton.

BACK, FRONT and SLEEVES
Follow the instructions for the body and sleeves of the sweater in Designer Tweed (p68).

INSERT PATTERN

The short row technique is used, worked as follows:

CAR, T3, carr set to H; bring all Ns to HP except 6 at R. K 6rs.

Push 3Ns at L to UWP, K to L.

Push 3Ns at R to HP. K 9rs.

Repeat to last 6sts. K 8rs. CAL. Weight and hold down the work as you knit.

JOINING SWEATER ARMHOLES

With wrong side of work facing, pick up 31sts from armhole edge of one body section, putting 2sts on one N at armhole edge. Knit insert pattern ending CAL. Do not break yarn.

Join in WY, K several rs and strip from machine. Re-hang work with right side facing.

With wrong side of one sleeve facing, matching neck and underarm, hang sleeve armhole sts onto corresponding Ns. K 1r T10, COff loosely using split stitch technique (see Techniques).

Join the remaining sections in the same way, making sure to pick up on the body section, knit the insert, then cast off after joining the sleeve.

NECKBAND (knitted in two sections)

Front neck:

★ CO 54sts 'E' wrap method (see Techniques).

K 4rs T4, 1r T8.

Join in sweater at neckline:

With wrong side of garment facing, pick up neckline sts from WY as follows, decreasing 16sts evenly across the work by putting 2sts on a N as necessary: 10sts onto 7Ns from each half of the sleeve top; 6sts onto 4Ns from top of each insert; 38sts onto 32Ns of front. 54sts. K 3rs T3. CAR.

Work insert pattern, ending CAL. K 3rs T2 across all sts. Do not break yarn.

Put work onto several rs WY and strip from machine. Reduce Ns to 46, and re-hang work, decreasing evenly across Ns.

K 5rs T4, 1r T8. Break yarn and leave on several rs WY. (Do not cast off yet or you will not be able to hang the back neck sts onto the Ns.)

Back neck:

The body is shaped at the neck edge before working the insert pattern.

With wrong side of work facing, pick up 70 neckline sts (same as front, without decreasing).

Set carr to HP. CAR.

Bring Ns 12-35 at L to HP, K to L.

Bring N11 at L to HP, Ns 12-35 at R to HP, K to R.

Push 11Ns at L to UWP, K to L.

Bring last N knitted at L to HP, push 11Ns at R to UWP, K to R.

Continue shaping in groups of 10, plus 1N for wrapping the yarn to avoid a hole in the work, until 5Ns remain at either end. K these back to WP on the last 2rs. CAR. Break yarn. K several rs WY and strip from machine.

Work as for front neck from ★, but finally COff with the latch tool after last r, T8.

Pick up sts on WY of front neck, and COff with the latch tool.

MAKING UP

Finish off ends using the latch tool. Damp press, omitting the welts and the insert bands at armholes and neckline. Steam the ribs as for Designer Tweed. Using sewing cotton, mattress-stitch ribs, backstitch underarm seams. Join neckbands neatly at shoulders. Press seams.

AFRICAN WEAVE SWEATERS

T HE INSPIRATION FOR THIS DESIGN came from a collection of African textiles in the British Museum, Museum of Mankind. Amongst resist-dyed, stencilled cloths, patchwork and embroidery are woven fabrics for traditional clothes and mats. The weaving is often done in narrow strips on homemade looms, and the strips joined to give whatever size fabric piece is required. The source for this design is a chequerboard cloth from Sierra Leone.

The geometric pattern, and the narrow repeats, made an easy translation to the knitting machine. However, in the transposition various changes had to take place. The knitting machine, with its own disciplines and techniques, dictates that you cannot copy a design slavishly from another craft. This is just as well, since the knitter is supposed to be inspired, though the temptation to copy a really lovely design is very strong. By the time the inspiration has been tempered or expanded by the knitting machine's capabilities it has developed new characteristics.

Because of the long verticals in the design, which would open the knitted fabric if it was worked in the single-bed Fair Isle technique, the double-bed jacquard technique seemed to be the solution. But this gave too 'industrial' a result for personal taste so a compromise was sought, and found by using selected needles only on the ribber: the ladder-backed technique discussed in Chapter 3. This gave a lighter and more pliable fabric. It was also possible to delineate the design rather than break it by organising the ribber needles to run up the verticals. Because the pattern repeat is 24sts wide and is organised in groups of four stitches, the design and its technical application were in total harmony. A long pattern card gave greater variety, and the final decision to Swiss-darn random areas gave a feeling of freedom to an otherwise formal geometric design.

The second style differs from the first at the armhole, both in shape and pattern detail. Increases were made after the welts on body and sleeve to produce a fuller look to the second sweater.

Background illustration taken from *African Textiles* by Christopher Spring. The original textile rests in The Museum of Mankind (registration number 1956. AF 10.9)

1 This sample is worked in 2/21 count, 4-ply equivalent Shetland yarn, tension 7. It served to test whether the design was good enough to use, and whether it was improved by areas of Swiss darning. The knitted fabric is, however, inflexible, though this could be improved by a looser tension. It was not the result looked for, so a finer yarn was selected

2 The unadorned sample in 4-ply equivalent botany yarn, the yarn finally chosen for the sweater because it knits up soft and flexible, and is perfect for the ladder-backed technique. The machine stitching for the cut-and-sew neckline was tested on this sample

3 Instead of choosing black for the second colour, it seemed more subtle to select a very dark bottle green: almost black, but not quite. The colours chosen for the decoration are incorporated in the welt, and a second design developed as a simple border pattern. The muted tones were achieved by using a soft fuchsia and dark mustard

4 Keeping the dark green of the second colour, the main colour, a light cream, takes the place of the buttery cream main colour in sample 3. This gives a lively colouring, further lifted by the bright Indian red and mustard of the decorative colours

5 The collar. This sample was discarded because a knot had passed by unnoticed on the cast-on row. Nevertheless, a lesson was learnt: the folded rib chosen for the garment gives a more professional finish at the neckline than a single thickness. The white rows (waste yarn), after the mustard and rust rounds of circular knitting, are carefully unravelled after pressing. The neckband then envelops the neckline of the sweater and is backstitched through the free stitches of the last circular row. This is the perfect neckband technique for a cut-and-sew neckline, and this design a perfect 'starter' if you have never dared to take scissors to knitted fabric before

Bright Tones

Though both these sweaters are in 'warm' colours, they would be equally successful in other colour combinations – blue variations, or a combination of green and blue on white and grey, perhaps

. . . .

Soft Shades

The way the armhole is shaped here is an invitation to use the border pattern at the top of the sleeve

. . . .

Bright Tones

YARN

Rowan Botany 100% Pure New Wool. 3/12 worsted count. 1kg/36oz = 4600m/5060yd approx.
1×350gm/12oz cone shade 649, light cream; col 1 (MY).
1×350gm/12oz cone shade 520, dark bottle; col 2.
100gm/3½oz shade 9, mustard; col 3.
100gm/3½oz shade 45, rust red; col 4.

MACHINE

Standard punchcard or electronic with ribber and optional colour changer. If not using a colour changer when working the ladder-backed jacquard, the yarns will be changed manually at the right side of the machine every two rows. Instructions are given assuming use of a colour changer.

PUNCHCARD MACHINES

You will need 4 punchcards to work the main design (see pages 78-9), so it could be simpler to use a continuous roll. Remember to start and finish with two fully punched rows to join, and be care-

ful to punch the two holes at either side for the clips in the correct place for pattern 2. Copy the placing from a standard punchcard.

TENSION

M/T/6/3, giving 32sts and 36rs to a 10cm/4in square. The number of sts includes those Ns at NWP on the MB. Rib tension: 2/2.
Because 2 passes of the carriage are necessary for one complete row in double jacquard knitting, the row counter will record double the number of rows knitted, eg the 60rs to be measured on the tension square will record as 120.
The close-knit bar should be used, and can remain in position throughout.
The half-pitch level is on H throughout.

MEASUREMENTS

Length 63cm/25in; chest 116cm/46in; sleeve length 51cm/20in.

RIBS

Arrange Ns for 2×1 rib. Set cols 1, 2 and 3 in the changer, and col 4 in the carriage. Using col 4, CO and work selvedge rs and 1r of rib, ending CAL. (K 1 more r of rib if changing cols manually at the right.)
RC000, K (2rs col 3, 2rs col 1) 8 times. K 2rs col 3. CAL, RC34.
Bring all empty Ns to WP on MB.

BACK and FRONT (both alike)

CO 186sts. Work rib as above. Arrange Ns for ladder-backed jacquard as follows:
Make sure that N13 to the left of centre O on the ribber has a stitch. Using this as a marker, arrange RB sts so that every 4th N has a st. N12 on MB should be to the right of N13 on RB; if not, check half-pitch lever. Transfer sts to MB or move to next N as necessary.
Set pattern 1 on r1. RC000, K as follows:

PATTERN 1   *Border Punchcard*

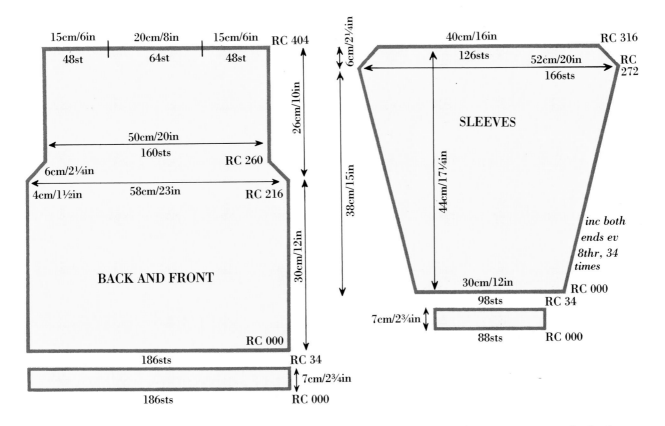

(2rs col 3, 2rs col 4, 2rs col 3, 2rs col 1) twice.
2rs col 3, 2rs col 4. CAL RC20.
Change to pattern 2, and K 2rs col 1, 2rs col 2, throughout.
K to RC216. Mark each end of r with a length of contrast yarn.
Following the RC recording, and not the actual rs knitted, dec 2sts FF at each end of next and foll 4th r, and 1st at each end of every foll 4th r, 9 times. K 1r. 160sts. RC258.
K to RC404.
Transfer RB sts to MB and leave on several rs of WY. Strip from machine.

SLEEVES (both alike)
CO 88sts. Work rib as above to RC34. CAL.
Transfer ribber sts to MB. K 1r col 3, T6.
K several rs WY and strip from machine. Remove comb and weights.
Push up to WP 5 more Ns each end. 98 Ns.
Replace rib, increasing 10sts evenly across work. (see Techniques). Remove WY carefully.
Arrange Ns for ladder-backed jacquard as above, transferring the heel of MB st to RB. Lower RB one stage and replace comb *behind* ribber Ns.
Raise RB to knitting position. Hang weights.
Check that all RB needles are in front of the comb.

Following colour and pattern sequence for back and front, inc both ends every foll 8th r 34 times.
166sts. RC272. Mark each end of r with a length of coloured yarn.
Dec 2st FF both ends next and every foll 4th r, 10 times altogether. K 7rs. 126sts. RC316. Transfer RB sts to MB. K several rs WY. Strip from machine.

JOIN SHOULDERS ON MACHINE
Push 48Ns to WP. With right side of one body section facing, pick up one set of shoulder sts. With wrong side of other body section facing, pick up matching shoulder sts onto same Ns. K 1r T10. COff with the latch tool.
Push 43Ns to WP. Omitting 5sts at neck edge, pick up and finish the second shoulder seam as the first.

NECKBAND
CO 196sts col 4. 2×1 rib. After circular rs, RC000, K 7rs T2/1, 6rs T1··/1, 10rs T1/1, RC23. K (2rs col 3, 2rs col 1) 4 times, 2rs col 3. *At the same time* change the tension as follows: 6rs T1/1, 6rs T1··/1, 6rs T2/1. RC41.
Bring empty Ns to WP on both beds for FNR.

PATTERN 1 *Mylar sheet*

PATTERN 2 *Mylar sheet*

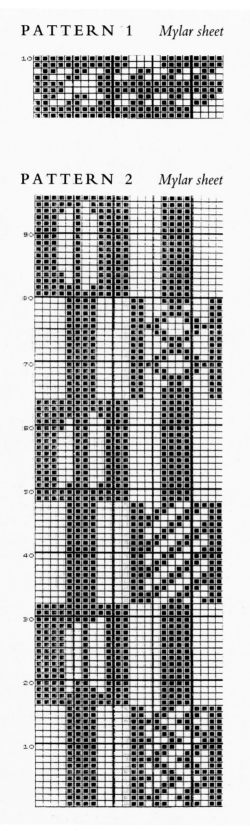

PATTERN 2 *Punchcard*

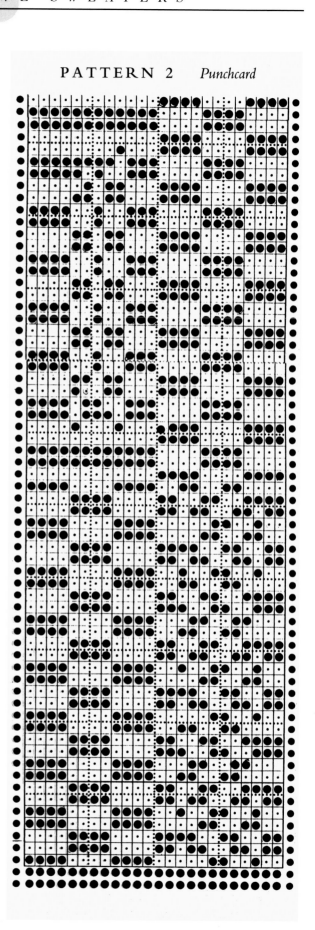

Full instructions for knitting the ladder-backed jacquard technique using both punchcard and mylar sheet are given in Chapter 3

PATTERN 2   *Punchcard*

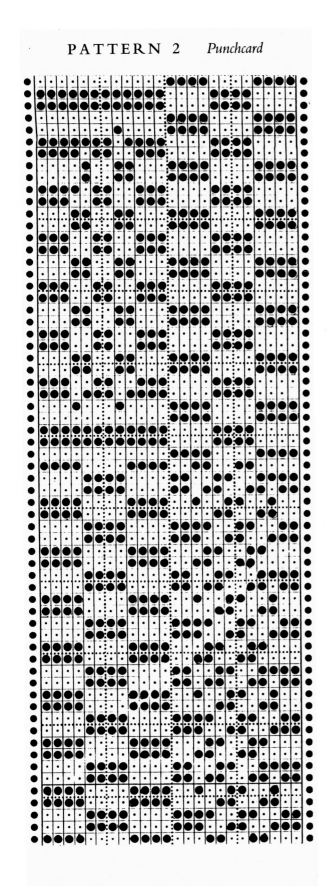

PATTERN 2   *Punchcard*

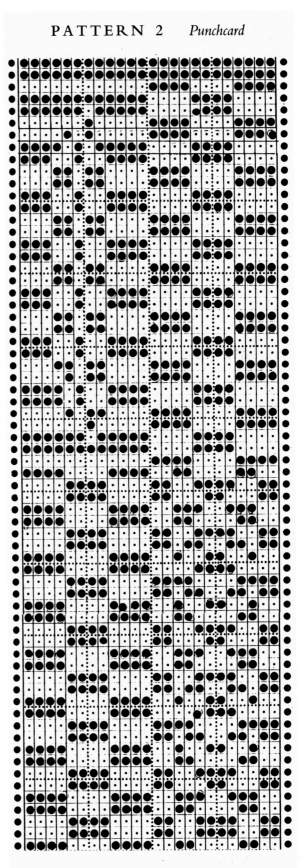

K 1r col 4 T2/1. CAR. Break yarn.
Set carrs to slip/part/free-move and take to L of machine. Set to K tubular, T6/6. K (2 rounds col 4, 2 rounds col 3) twice, K 2 rounds col 4 (2 rounds = 4 carriage movements). CAL. Set carr for FNR. Join in WY. K several rs WY.
Strip carefully from machine.

MAKING UP

JOIN SLEEVE TO ARMHOLE ON MACHINE
Push 166Ns to WP.
With right side of sleeve facing, coloured marker at end Ns, pick up 126 sts from WY, and 20 from each armhole shaping.
With wrong side of body facing, shoulder seam at centre O, coloured markers at end Ns, pick up 126sts evenly on the straight, keeping to the same line of sts, 2sts in from edge. Pick up 20 from each armhole shaping. Weave in ends (see Techniques). K 1r T10, COff with the latch tool.
Press garment and neckband, excluding all ribs.

Steam ribs by holding iron close to rib but not pressing.
Lie garment flat, preferably pinning to a suitable surface. Using templates (see Techniques) mark neckline with tacking sts.
Work 2 rs of zig-zag machine sts or 2 lines of hand backstitch immediately within the tacking sts, and cut away the surplus knitted fabric. Secure the free sts at one shoulder with a length of yarn. Remove the WY from the neckband carefully. (The sts will be fixed by pressing and will not run).
Lay the neckband over the neck edge, slipping the ends over the 5 free shoulder sts, and pin in place. With right side of garment facing, backstitch evenly through the loops using col 4. Backstitch the loops on the wrong side into place. Mattress-stitch the neckband seam at open shoulder. Fold neckband to inside and slip-stitch to row of FNR. If you are intending to Swiss darn, this is easier to work before finishing the garment seams.
Finally, mattress stitch all rib seams, and backstitch underarm and body seams 2sts in, keeping to the same line of sts. Give a final pressing.

· · · · · · · · · · · · · · · · · · ·

Soft Shades

●●●●●●●●●●●●●●●●●●●●●●

YARN
As for style 1, quantities and shades as follows:
1×350gm/12oz cone shade 6, dark cream; col 1 (MY).
1×350gm/12oz cone shade 520, dark bottle; col 2.
100gm/3½oz shade 70, fuchsia; col 3.
100gm/3½oz shade 521, dark mustard; col 4.

MACHINE
As for style 1.

TENSION
As for style 1.

MEASUREMENTS
As for style 1.

RIBS
Work as style 1 up to RC34, but colour sequence is as follows:
CO col 3, working the selvedge rs and 1st r, ending CAL if using the colour changer. Knit 1 more r if changing cols manually, ending CAR.
K (2rs col 4, 2rs col 1) 8 times. K 2rs col 4. CAL RC34.
Transfer ribber sts to MB, and K 1r T6. Finish on WY and strip from the machine. Remove comb and weights.

BACK and FRONT (both alike)
Push 170Ns to WP. Knit rib as above.
Push 186Ns to WP. Hang rib onto Ns, increasing 16sts evenly across the Ns (see Techniques).

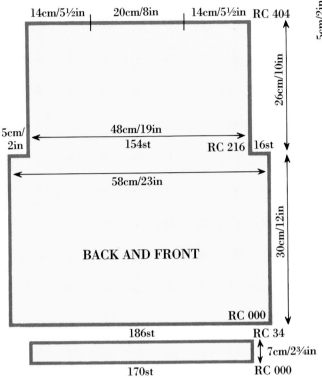

14cm/5½in 20cm/8in 14cm/5½in RC 404

26cm/10in

5cm/2in 48cm/19in 154st RC 216 16st

58cm/23in

30cm/12in

BACK AND FRONT

RC 000

186st RC 34

7cm/2¾in

170st RC 000

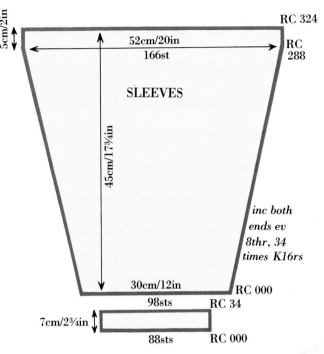

5cm/2in RC 324

52cm/20in RC 288
166st

SLEEVES

45cm/17¾in

inc both ends ev 8thr, 34 times K16rs

30cm/12in RC 000
98sts RC 34

7cm/2¾in

88sts RC 000

Carefully remove WY. Arrange Ns for ladder-backed jacquard (see style 1). Lower RB one stage and hang cast-on comb *behind* ribber Ns. Raise RB to knitting position. Hang weights.

Set pattern 1 on r1. RC000, change colours as follows: K (2rs col 1, 2rs col 3, 2rs col 1, 2rs col 4) twice; 2rs col 1, 2rs col 3. RC20.

Change to pattern 2, knitting 2rs col 1, 2rs col 2 throughout, K to RC216.

COff 16sts at beg of next 2rs (154sts) K to RC404. Transfer RB sts to MB.

Leave on several rs WY and strip from machine. Join shoulders on machine (as style 1).

SLEEVES

CO 88sts, and K rib the same as back and front, increasing to 98sts (as style 1).

Arrange Ns for ladder-backed jacquard (as before).

Following pattern and colour sequence for back and front, increase both ends every 8th r, 34 times, K 16rs. RC288.

Change to pattern 1 and colour sequence as follows:
★K (2rs col 1, 2rs col 3, 2rs col 1, 2rs col 4)★ twice, 2rs col 1, 2rs col 3.

Starting at 3rd r of pattern 1: 2rs col 1, 2rs col 4.

Repeat from ★ to ★ once more; 2rs col 1, 2rs col 3. RC324. Transfer RB sts to MB. Leave on several rs WY and strip from machine.

NECKBAND

Work as for style 1, but changing colours as follows:
CO col 3 and work to RC23.

K (2rs col 4, 2rs col 1) 4 times, 2rs col 4. RC41.

Bring empty Ns to WP on both beds, T2/1, K 1r col 4.

Set carr to K tubular.

T6/6 K (2 rounds col 3, 2 rounds col 4) twice, 2 rounds col 3. (2 rounds=4carriage movements).

Finish as style 1.

MAKING UP

Follow instructions as for style 1, joining the cast off sts at underarm to pattern 1 section at sleeve top.

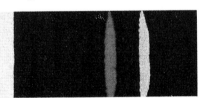

SPORTS SWEATERS

THE STYLE OF THIS SWEATER, with its classic collar and tab front, is nothing new. Made in botany wool, cotton, cotton/linen mix, mixtures of natural and manmade fibres, it is found everywhere, from the most expensive store to the market stall. There have always been one or two in my family, belonging to no-one in particular and worn by everyone in their turn, being so useful and so popular.

With a style so much in demand, it was not long before the machine knitter among us was called upon to produce replicas. Devising the pattern was easy enough: an original was measured, the measurements transferred to dress-maker's paper (marked in centimetre squares) and thence onto the sheet of the charting device. The first homemade affair was soon modified, and lessons learnt at the same time: increasing after knitting welts and cuffs was one improvement, grading the tensions of the collar was another. And full needle rib for the collar and buttonhole band was essential for a professional finish.

The formal and linear two-colour design used here is a development of fleeting impression of plain glazing seen in a church. Outside, the rain was blown against the panes in squally gusts, and though it was a grey and cold early spring day, the plain glass windows set in fine stonework, and divided by finer iron horizontals and grey-black leading, gave an airy lightness to the church interior. It was a long time before the impression found its way onto paper, but the visual memory was so strong that no preliminary drawings were needed; it was planned directly onto stitch-related graph paper, a card was punched and in no time the samples were produced. It was inevitably called 'Rainy Windows'.

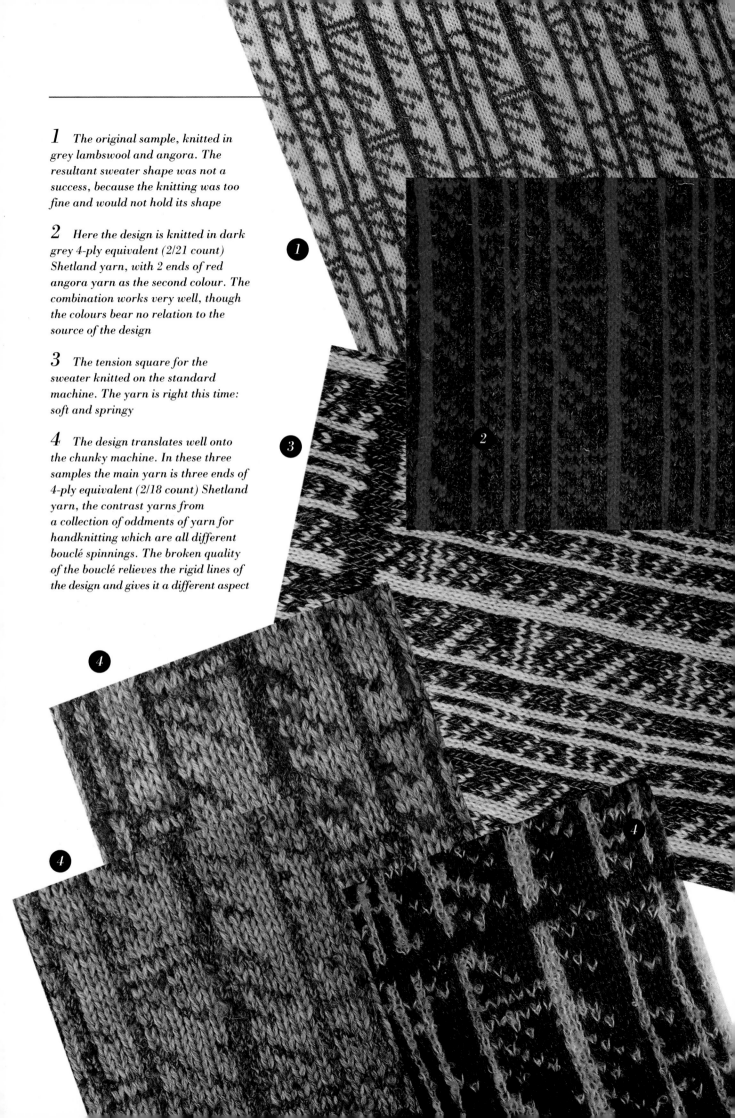

1   The original sample, knitted in grey lambswool and angora. The resultant sweater shape was not a success, because the knitting was too fine and would not hold its shape

2   Here the design is knitted in dark grey 4-ply equivalent (2/21 count) Shetland yarn, with 2 ends of red angora yarn as the second colour. The combination works very well, though the colours bear no relation to the source of the design

3   The tension square for the sweater knitted on the standard machine. The yarn is right this time: soft and springy

4   The design translates well onto the chunky machine. In these three samples the main yarn is three ends of 4-ply equivalent (2/18 count) Shetland yarn, the contrast yarns from a collection of oddments of yarn for handknitting which are all different bouclé spinnings. The broken quality of the bouclé relieves the rigid lines of the design and gives it a different aspect

Standard

Here the sweater is knitted in industrial yarn. Both yarns are obviously luxury yarns and, bought from a mill clearance, cost a fraction of their true worth, so they are very economical and, what is more, exciting to knit with. The pattern is given exactly as I worked it out for this yarn. · Should you be fortunate enough to make a similar find, you will be involved in working out rows and stitches for the design from your own tension square. The rule with yarns like these is to play about with tension, stitch and pattern until you get everything right: the stitch design looks good, the knitted fabric feels soft and pliable – not too loose or too tight a tension – and the overall effect is in harmony with what you are planning to knit

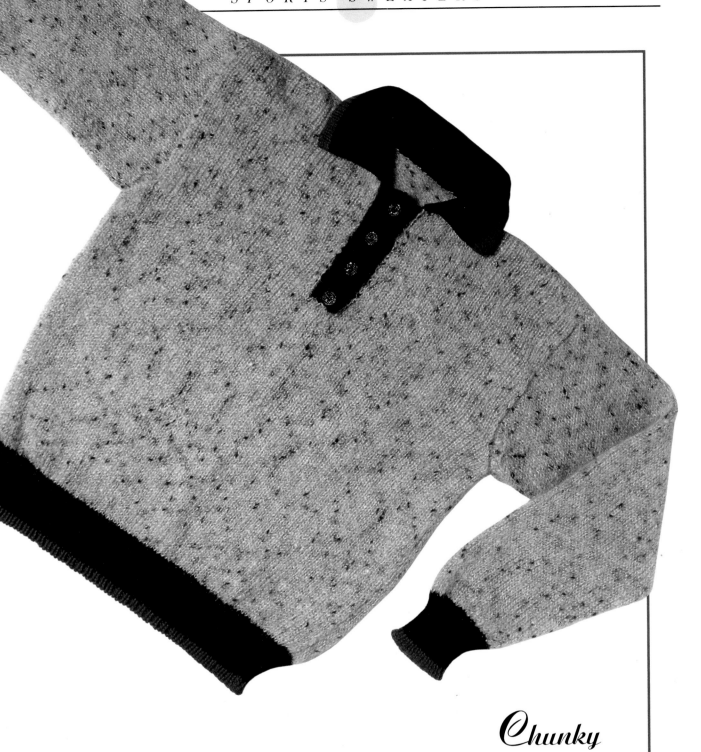

Chunky

The final choice of mohair for
this sweater was difficult – there
are so many tempting colours.
The decision to knit welts and
collar in a plain woollen yarn
proved sensible on two counts:
some wearers find mohair too
tickly near the face but, more
importantly, the contrast welts
made it possible to knit the
sweater using only one cone of
the main, mohair yarn

Chunky

YARN

Yorkshire Mohair Mills Italian Collection Gold
Award Mohair. 50gm/2oz = 100m/110yd.
1×450gm/15oz cone shade 1054; MY.
Yorkshire Mohair Mills Highland Aran.
50gm/1¾oz = 100m/110yd. 100gm/3oz black.
Approx 25gm/1oz contrast for edging. (A ball of
chunky for handknitting is used here, col. fuchsia.)
Sweater uses 420gm/15oz main yarn.

MACHINE

Chunky with ribber.

TENSION

MT4, giving 16sts and 24rs to a 10cm/4in square.

MEASUREMENTS

Length: 64cm/25in; chest: 112cm/44in; sleeve
length, 52cm/20in (shoulder is dropped, shortening
sleeve length).

BACK

Welt: CO 82sts in edging contrast. Work circular
selvedge rs, and 2rs T2/2, change to black yarn.
K 18rs. Break yarn, transfer ribber sts to MB. K
several rs WY and strip from machine.
Push up 5 extra Ns at either side. 92Ns. Re-hang
rib sts, increasing evenly across work.
Join in mohair yarn and K T4 to RC72. CAR.
Mark end sts with a length of coloured yarn.
Dec 1st at both ends next and alt rs 6 times in all★.
K to RC134. Leave sts on WY.

FRONT

Work as for back to ★. Divide for front opening:
Bring 37Ns at L to HP. Put centre 6sts onto a
length of contrast yarn. Set carr to H.
Knitting on 37sts at R, weighting L edge of
knitting to prevent tightening work, K to RC122.
CAR.
Set carr to HP.
Push 2Ns at L to HP, K to L.

Push last N knitted to HP, K to R.
Push 1N at neck edge to HP on the foll 10rs. 24sts.
RC134.
Put shoulder sts onto several rs WY, strip from
machine.
Push neckline sts to UWP. K 1r MY, T4.
Work several rs WY. Strip from machine. (The r
of MY prevents loss of sts when picking up for the
collar.)
Work L front to match, starting with CAL.

SLEEVES (both alike)

CO 42sts, and work as for body welts, increasing to
48sts. Join in mohair. Inc both ends every 4th r 20
times. K 12rs straight. 88sts. RC92. Mark end sts
with a length of coloured yarn. Dec 1st at both
ends of next 12rs. 64sts. RC104. Leave sts on WY.

JOIN SHOULDERS

This is done on the machine: Push 24Ns to WP.

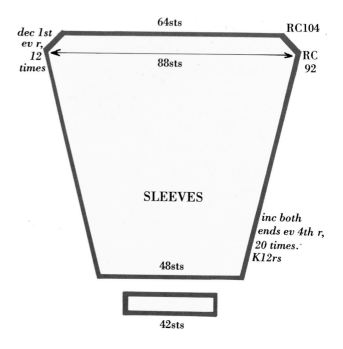

dec 1st ev r, 12 times · 64sts · RC104 · 88sts · RC92 · SLEEVES · inc both ends ev 4th r, 20 times. K12rs · 48sts · 42sts

With R side of garment back facing, replace one set of shoulder sts from WY onto the Ns. With wrong side of garment front facing, replace matching shoulder sts. K 1r T10, COff with the latch tool. Finish the second shoulder to match.

JOIN SLEEVES TO ARMHOLE

This is also done on the machine: Push 80Ns to WP. With R side of sleeve facing, pick up 8sts from each underarm shaping starting at the coloured marker, and 64 from sleeve top. 80sts. With wrong side of garment body facing, shoulder seam at centre O, coloured marker at N40 either side, pick up 64sts evenly along armhole edge, 1st in, taking care to follow the same line of sts, and 8sts from each armhole shaping, bringing Ns to HP as you do so. Weave in ends (see Techniques). K 1r T10. COff with the latch tool. Join second armhole seam the same.

COLLAR

This is worked in full needle rib: Push 64Ns on MB, 66 on RB to WP. The outside Ns should be on ribber.

CO in edging contrast, and work 3 circular selvedge rs. CAR. Now transfer sts 2 and 3 on RB to Ns 1 and 2 of MB at each end. Push empty Ns to NWP.

Knit, changing tension as follows:
T3·, K 2rs. Break yarn, join in black, K 4rs.
T2··, K 6rs.
T2, K 6rs.
T1·, K6rs.
Transfer ribber sts to MB.

JOIN NECK TO COLLAR

With wrong side of garment neck facing, and increasing 6 sts by picking up the heel of 2sts from back and each front, pick up the neckline sts and put onto corresponding collar Ns.
Bring Ns to HP as you do this (it makes the next row easier to knit). K 3rs T4, 1r T10. COff with the latch tool. (This is the neck facing).

TAB FRONT

With black yarn CO 6sts FNR (use edge wires and small weights to weight work).
Work buttonhole section first:
T2/2, work buttonholes on rs3, 15, 27 and 39 as follows:
After knitting buttonhole r, transfer st on N1 at R of centre O on MB to N1 to R of O on ribber; st on N1 at L of O on ribber to N1 to L of O on MB. Leave empty Ns at WP and continue knitting. After all buttonholes have been worked, K 3rs. RC42. K 1r T6/6, K 42rs T2/2.

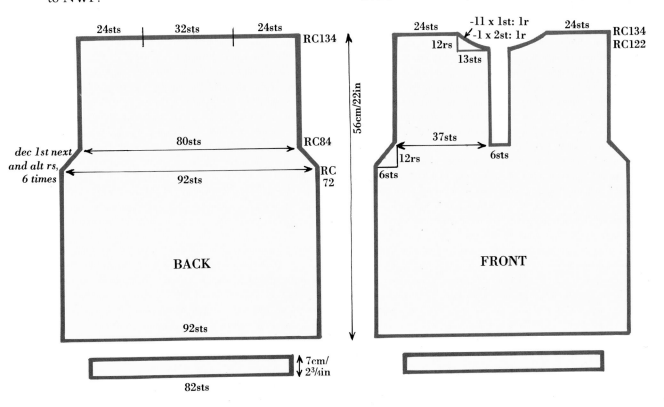

Break yarn. Leave work on several *circular* rs WY.

MAKING UP

Finish neckline first: catch-stitch neck collar facing to body, using MY.

Finish tab front as follows: fold back WY and graft sts (see Techniques).

Fold tab front on T6/6 r, and join to 6sts at centre front. With R side of work facing, join buttonhole edge to garment using mattress stitch so that buttons will fasten to L or R as preferred.
Join other edge the same.

Mattress-stitch welts in appropriate colours, and backstitch underarm seams in MY. Finally, damp-press seams with iron set for wool, and lightly steam ribs without pressing. The main garment can be very lightly pressed if wished.

. . . .

Standard

●●●●●●●●●●●●●●●●●●●●●

YARN

This sweater is made from industrial yarn.
The main yarn (MY) is an unspecified mixture, probably wool and mohair, count 3/24, using 1 end: 230gm/8oz. (2 ends were used for welts, but not for collar and tab front.) The contrast yarn is angora Tex 12, using 2 ends throughout: 180gm/6oz. The alpaca/lambswool mix supplied by Celandine would give a very similar result, using 2 ends throughout.

You quickly get to grips with the basic elements of machine knitting when you use un-named industrial yarns. There is no suggested tension, no yarn quantity given, no pattern to rely on as a starting point. Nothing will give you more confidence and know-how than working it all out for yourself. The main yarn used in this design has very light grey flecks in it when knitted up, which soften the contrast and relieve what could be a very rigid design.
Nothing on the inside of the cone revealed its content, but it feels soft and luxurious, revealing exotic long hairs on washing.

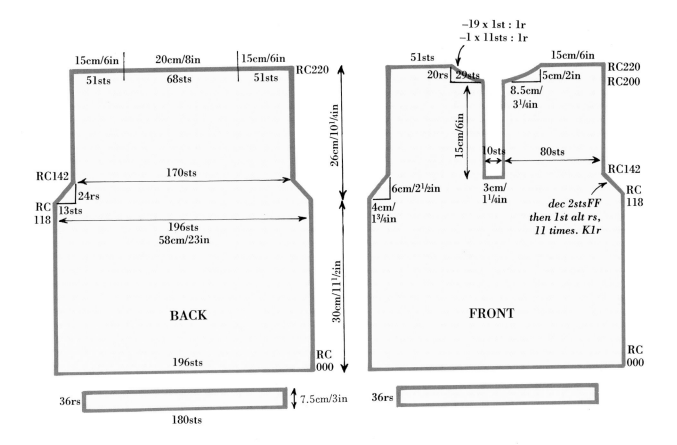

BACK

15cm/6in 20cm/8in 15cm/6in
51sts 68sts 51sts RC220

26cm/10¼in

RC142 170sts
24rs
RC 118 13sts
196sts
58cm/23in

30cm/11½in

BACK

196sts RC 000

36rs 7.5cm/3in
180sts

FRONT

−19 x 1st : 1r
−1 x 11sts : 1r

51sts
20rs 29sts RC220
RC200
5cm/2in
8.5cm/3¼in

15cm/6in

6cm/2½in
4cm/1¾in
10sts 3cm/1¼in 80sts

15cm/6in
RC142
RC 118

dec 2stsFF then 1st alt rs, 11 times. K1r

FRONT

RC 000

36rs

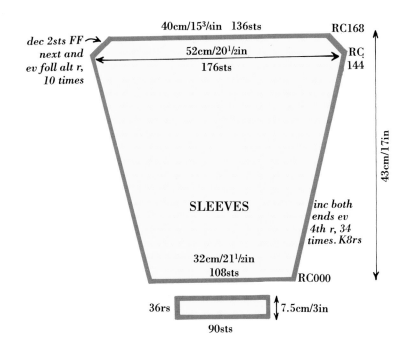

40cm/15¾in 136sts RC168
dec 2sts FF next and ev foll alt r, 10 times
52cm/20½in RC 144
176sts

43cm/17in

SLEEVES

inc both ends ev 4th r, 34 times. K8rs

32cm/21½in
108sts RC000

36rs 7.5cm/3in
90sts

STANDARD *Punchcard*

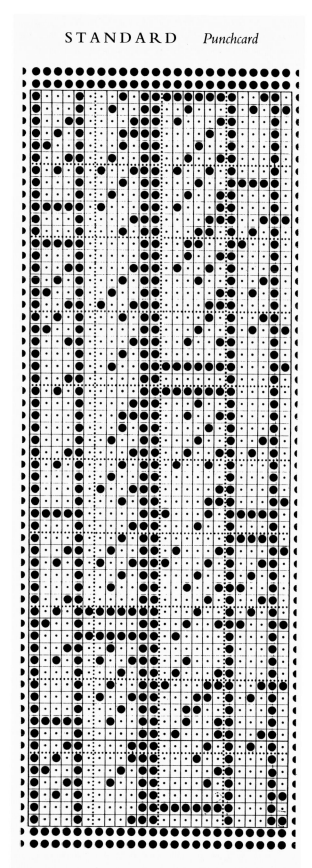

MACHINE
Standard machine with ribber.

TENSION
MT6, giving 34sts and 39rs to a 10cm/4in square after washing and pressing.

MEASUREMENTS
As for the Chunky sweater.

WELTS
Knit the welts first, leaving on WY.

BODY WELTS
CO 180sts in contrast. Work circular selvedge rs and 2rs T1/1.
Change to 2 ends MY and K 34rs. Transfer ribber sts to MB. Leave sts on WY.

CUFFS
CO 90sts in contrast, knit and finish as for welts.

BACK
Push up 196Ns on MB. Pick up last r of rib, increasing 16sts evenly across the Ns (see Techniques). R000, MT6, K in pattern to RC118. Mark each end of r with a length of coloured yarn.
Shape armholes:
Using the triple-ended transfer tool, dec 2sts FF each end of next r. Still using the same transfer tool, dec 1st each end of every alt r 11 times. K1r. CAR. RC142. 170sts.★ K to RC220.
Leave sts on 3 groups of WY: 51sts for each shoulder, 68 for back neck.

FRONT
Work as for back to ★. Memorise card/mylar sheet row number.
Push 90Ns at L to HP. Set carr to H. Finish R side first.
Being careful to weight L edge to prevent tightening, K to RC200. CAR.
Shape front neck:
Push 10Ns to HP at neck edge. K to L.
Push last N knitted to HP. K to R.
Push 1N to HP at neck edge on every r 18 times. 51sts. RC220. Put shoulder sts onto several rs WY. Strip from machine. Push neckline sts to UWP.
K 1r MY, T6. Work several rs of WY. Strip from machine. (The row of MY prevents loss of sts when picking up for the collar.)

Leave 10sts at centre on a length of contrast yarn.
Replace sts at L to WP using a transfer tool.
Carr set for slip/free-move/part, no yarn in feeder,
re-set memorised pattern row from R to L. Re-set
RC to 142, and K L front to match R front,
reversing shapings.

SLEEVES (both alike)

Push up 108Ns on MB. Pick up last r of cuff rib,
increasing 18sts evenly across the sts.
RC000, MT6, K in pattern, inc both ends every
4th r 34 times. RC136. 176sts. K 8rs straight.
RC144. Mark each end of r with a length of
coloured yarn.
Shape armholes:
Using the triple-ended transfer tool, dec 2sts FF at
both ends of next and every foll alt r 10 times in
all. 136sts. RC164. K 4rs straight. RC168. Leave
on several rs WY.

JOIN SHOULDERS

See Chunky pattern, working on 51sts.

JOIN SLEEVES TO ARMHOLE

Push 176Ns to WP.
With right side of sleeve facing, pick up 136sts
from WY, and 20sts from each armhole shaping.
With wrong side of body facing, shoulder seam at
centre O, coloured marker at N88 each side, pick
up 136sts evenly along armhole edge, 1st in, taking
care to follow the same line of sts, and 20sts from
each armhole shaping, bringing the Ns out to HP
as you do so. Weave in all ends (see Techniques).
K 1r T10 and COff with the latch tool. Join
second armhole seam the same.

COLLAR

This is worked in FNR:
Push up 124Ns on MB, 126 on RB. The outside
Ns should be on ribber.

CO in contrast. Work circular selvedge rs. CAR.
Now transfer sts 2 and 3 of ribber to Ns 1 and 2 on
MB at each end. Push empty Ns to NWP. Knit,
changing tension as follows:
T2··, K 2rs. Break yarn, join in end MY.
T2··, K 10rs.
T2, K 12rs.
T1·, K 12rs.
T··, K 8rs.
Transfer RB sts to MB.

JOIN GARMENT NECK TO COLLAR

With wrong side of garment neck facing,
pick up the neckline sts and put them onto the
corresponding collar Ns. K 5rs T6, 1r T10. COff
with the latch tool. (This is the facing for the
neck.)

TAB FRONT

With MY CO 12sts FNR. (Use edge wires and
small weights to weight work.)
Work buttonhole section first:
T0/0, work buttonholes on rs6, 25, 44, 63 and 82
as for Chunky sweater.
When all buttonholes have been worked, K 8rs.
RC90. K 1r T6/6. K 90rs. Leave work on several
circular rs WY.

MAKING UP

Make up as for Chunky sweater, but mattress-stitch
body seams, keeping on the same line of sts
throughout. The sleeve seams can be backstitched.
If you have used industrial yarn in oil, wash the
sweater by hand in warm water and liquid
detergent. Washing-up liquid will do.
Spin, and then dry flat. Press garment as for
Chunky sweater.

CHUNKY JACKET

BEING EAGER TO COMBINE moss stitch with cables and not to knit what could be called a 'practical' cardigan, I decided to use the stitch combination for those areas of a classic cardigan that would normally be ribbed. This immediately has the effect of making the design slightly more sophisticated. The cardigan becomes a jacket. I also wanted a feminine design, so for this emphasis planned a set-in and slightly puffed sleeve.

Coincidentally, I had been sampling some chunky yarn that knitted smoothly in the machine, producing a really good-looking knitted fabric of obvious quality. What is more it was very strong - ideal for cabling. Although I had chosen to work this technique on the larger-gauge machine because it would produce results quickly, I was depressed at the length of time it took to produce the little sample seen here. But experience told me that practice would generate more speed and so, with slight misgivings, I went ahead and designed the jacket. Once embarked upon, the knitting grew faster than I had expected, and the prospect of the result I had envisaged kept the spirits up.

The jacket was worth it. So much so, that I went ahead and used it as the basis for an intarsia design originally planned for the standard machine.

1   This little sample was a practice piece for re-forming purl stitches to produce moss stitch. A fairly daunting task at first, but skill in working soon grows, making it a worthwhile technique to master

2   It is a good idea to try out a small area of intarsia if you have not used the technique before. Here I used the main yarn from the plain jacket, combined with some scraps of handknitting yarn

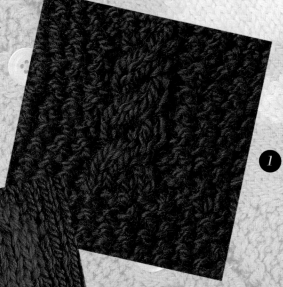

3   The motif for the front of the
intarsia jacket is adapted from a
Persian rug. Similar motifs appear on
Turkestan textiles. By the time it had
been drawn and altered to fit the area
on the knitting it had changed shape
considerably, mostly because there
were not enough rows on the Chunky
pattern to produce the more elaborate
shape originally planned for a
standard machine

4   A small template was made for the
main shape. This was then placed in
position on the stitch-related graph
paper and drawn around. The
resultant shape was then squared off
and simplified.
This design proved too intricate to
translate successfully to the high
tension needed for the chunky machine,
but it could easily be developed for the
standard gauge machine

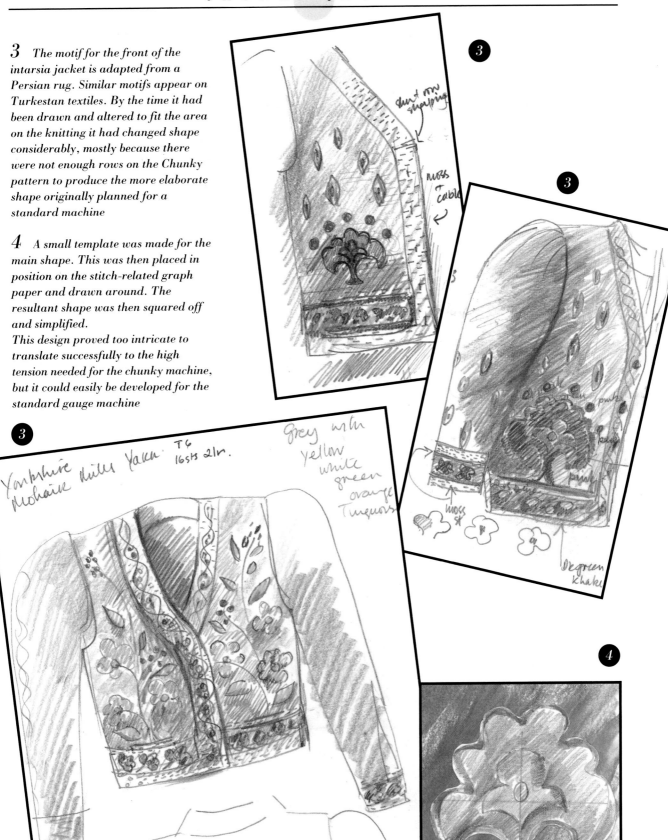

Chunky Jacket

Designed to rest on the hip line and to stand slightly away from the body, this jacket is gently shaped at the side seams. The front bands continue separately from the body after the moss and cable welts are knitted, and are sewn to the fronts when the knitting is finished. Pockets are partially concealed in the front welts

. . . .

Intarsia Jacket

The basic pattern for this jacket with intarsia decoration is identical to the plain jacket. Because the yarn is thick the tension is high, so the inlaid shapes have to be kept simple – but there is no loss in the decorative quality of the design

. . . .

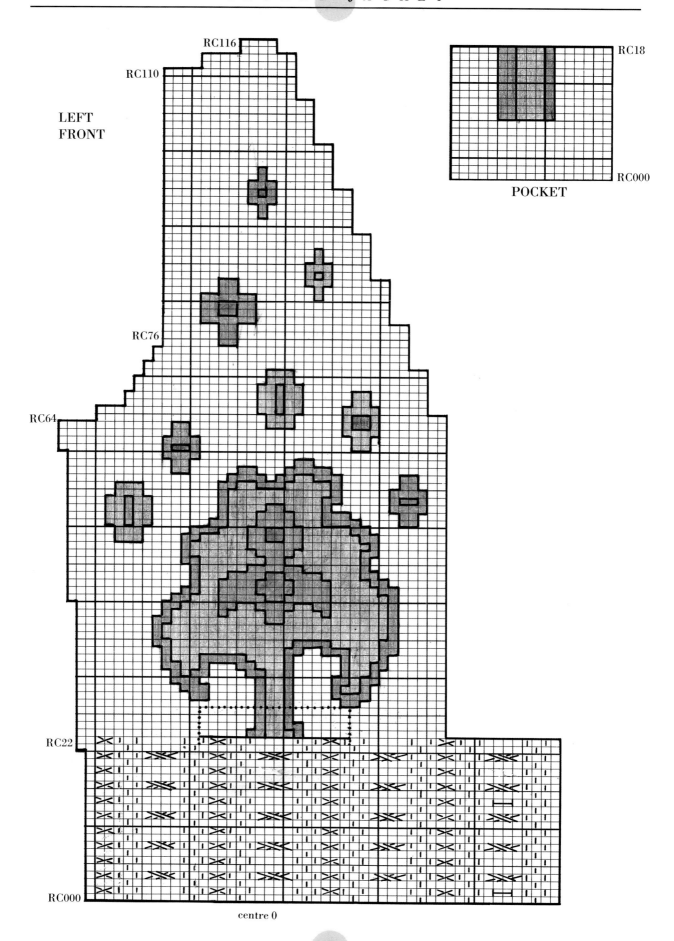

RC116
RC110

LEFT
FRONT

RC76

RC64

RC22

RC000

centre 0

RC18

POCKET

RC000

*It is a good idea to enlarge the charts on a photocopier
for ease of working. You will need to refer to the text
for pocket details, and for working the front bands*

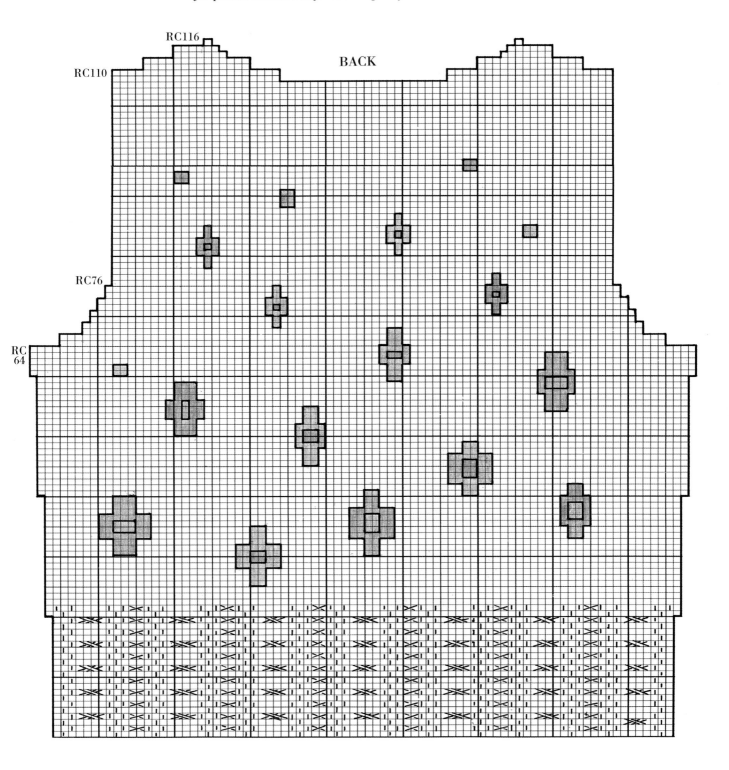

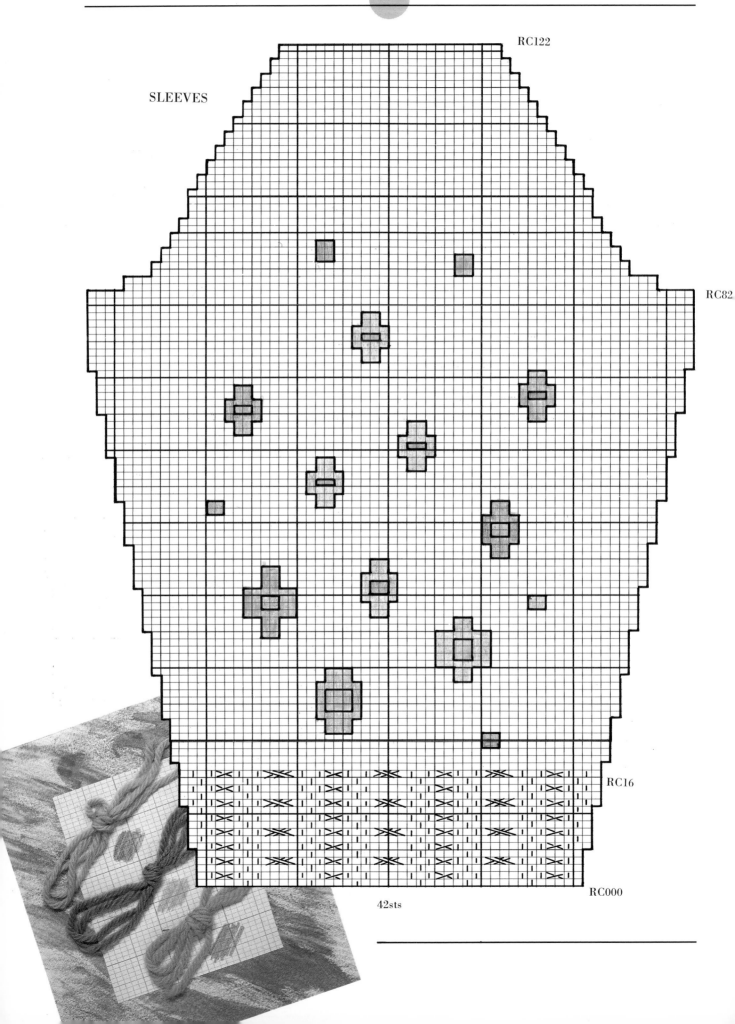

SLEEVES

RC122

RC82

RC16

RC000

42sts

READ THESE NOTES FOR BOTH DESIGNS

Cable and moss stitch borders:

Before starting to knit, mark the plastic strip or the metal of your needle bed on either side of the groups of 2 and 4Ns which will have the cable sts (see chart). The groups of 3sts between are moss stitch (alternating K and P sts). Use a chinagraph pencil for this; it will rub off easily when you are finished.

Follow the chart for re-forming for moss stitch and making cable crossings. Do not re-form end stitches. All casting on rows are made by the 'e' wrap method (see Techniques). After casting on, bring Ns out to HP and K them back to WP on the 1st r, to facilitate the knitting. Then hang cast-on comb (if available) and/or weights.

CAR, RC000, K 1r. Re-form the P sts on the 1st r according to chart – this will be the centre st in the moss st sections of the chart. Insert the latch tool into the st below the one on the needle. Push tool through and upwards until the st is behind the latch. Pull out the st in the N, allowing the loose strand to lie in hook. Pull the strand through the stitch and replace the K st thus formed onto the empty N. When re-forming and cabling, adopt a system of working. This helps to avoid mistakes, and also

helps to develop speed. The one that works well for me is as follows:

Knit the row; re-form all sts according to chart; cable blocks of 2sts, then cable blocks of 4sts according to the row number.

Bring the blocks of 4 cable st Ns out to HP, and knit them back on the next row after checking for errors.

The moss and cable front bands are not shown on the chart because of the difference in tension.

Any sts left on WY are cast off to prevent unravelling, except for those of pocket lining.

BUTTONHOLES

Buttonhole row:

Transfer the two centre sts of the cable, one to N at L, and one to N at R. Leave empty Ns at WP. K 1r. Insert single transfer tool down behind strand in L buttonhole N. Push N forward and back so that the latch closes and the strand comes off. Angling the point of the transfer tool slightly towards you, bring the handle down so that the tool is pointing upwards and the strand is 'e' wrapped around it. Transfer to empty N. Repeat for R buttonhole N. Bring both Ns to HP and K back on next r.

. . . .

Chunky Jacket

●●●●●●●●●●●●●●●●●●●●●

YARN

Yorkshire Mohair Mills Designer Chunky, 50gm/2oz = 50m/55yd.

Plain jacket: 800gm/29oz shade IW37, purple.

Intarsia jacket: 800gm/29oz shade IW35, denim, plus Yorkshire Mohair Mills Highland Aran, 50gm/2oz = 100m/110yd. 50gm/2oz each dusky pink and aqua. 100gm/4oz beige.

The contrast yarns are used double.

BUTTONS

7×25mm/1¼in max size.

MACHINE

Chunky machine without ribber. Intarsia carriage for the second jacket.

TENSION

MT6, giving 16sts and 21rs to a 10cm/4in square. Patterned border: 18sts and 22rs to a 10cm/4in square.

MEASUREMENTS

Length: 55cm/22in; chest: 108cm/42in; sleeve length: 55cm/22in.

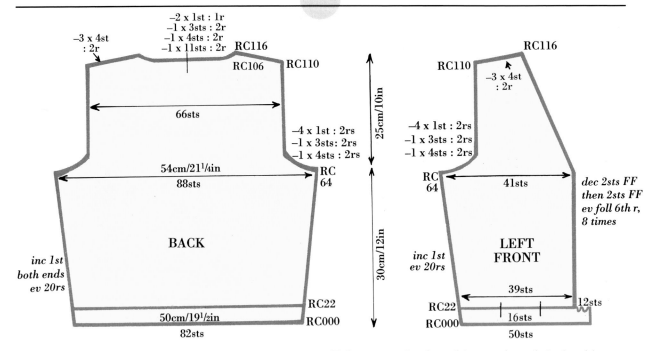

BACK

CO 82sts T6 (see Notes). Following chart, work to RC22, and then K to RC64, at the same time increasing at both ends every 20th r 3 times. 66sts.

ARMHOLES

COff 4sts at beg of next 2rs, 3sts at beg of following 2rs, and 1st both ends next and alt rs 4 times. Use triple transfer tool, moving 3sts 1st in. Push empty N back to NWP. K 1r. RC76. K 30rs. RC106. CAR.

SHAPE NECK AND SHOULDERS

Finish R side first: Set carr to H.
Bring all Ns at L and 9Ns at R of centre O to HP. K to L.
Bring last N knitted to HP, K to R.
Bring 3Ns at L to HP, K to L.
Bring last N knitted to HP, and 3Ns at R to HP, K to R.
Bring last N knitted at R to HP, and 2Ns at L to HP. K to L.
Bring last N knitted to HP and 3Ns at R to HP. K to R.
Bring last N knitted to HP, and 1N at L to HP. K to L.
Bring last N knitted to HP and 3Ns at R to HP, K to R.
Bring last N knitted to HP, and 1N at L to HP. K to L.
Bring final N at L to HP. RC116.
Push 12 shoulder sts to UWP. K 1r T8. Leave on WY.

Take carr to L of machine, and work L shoulder to match.
K 1r T8 on neckline sts and COff with the transfer tool, taking care not to tighten sts.

LEFT FRONT

Work pocket lining first: CO 'e' wrap 16 sts. K 18rs T6. Leave on WY.
Push up 50Ns to WP, start at N20 at L, ending N30 at R.
Increasing every 20th r at L work cable band as for back. After working r22, bring all Ns to HP except for 12 at R. Put these 12sts on WY and push empty Ns back to NWP.

POCKET OPENING

Push 8Ns either side of centre O to UWP.
With carr set to HP work on centre 16sts. Keep to pattern: work 3rs T6, 1r T10. COff with latch tool.
With wrong side of pocket lining facing, replace last r onto empty Ns. Remove WY. 39sts. CAR.
Re-set RC to 22. Work 42rs. RC64 CAR.
Shape armhole at left as for back. At the same time at R decrease 2sts FF (use the triple transfer tool, lifting 3sts 2sts in, pushing the 2 empty Ns to NWP) on next r and then every foll 6th r 8 times, shaping shoulder at RC110 following instructions for back.

FRONT BAND

Replace the 12 front band sts onto the centre 12Ns. The large cable is on the centre 4Ns, with 4 moss sts at either side.

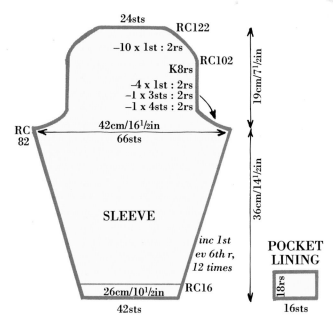

SLEEVE

24sts
RC122
−10 x 1st : 2rs
RC102
K8rs
−4 x 1st : 2rs
−1 x 3sts : 2rs
−1 x 4sts : 2rs
RC
82
42cm/16½in
66sts
19cm/7½in
36cm/14½in
inc 1st
ev 6th r,
12 times
26cm/10½in   RC16
42sts

**POCKET
LINING**
18rs
16sts

Continue in border pattern to RC78. CAR. Mark
L end of row with a length of contrast yarn.
Work 4 short rows to follow shaping of 'V' neck:
Set carr to HP.
Bring 2Ns at L to HP. K to L. Re-form sts at WP.
Bring last N knitted to HP. K to R. Re-form sts
at WP.
Repeat these 2rs, cabling on R80. 6Ns at L are at
WP. RC82 CAR.
Re-set RC to 78, knitting back Ns at HP to WP
on next r, and cabling again on r80. K 66rs.
RC144. Mark L end of r with a length of contrast
yarn (point of shoulder seam).
Work a further 30rs to centre back neck, RC174,
and leave sts on WY.

RIGHT FRONT
Push up 50Ns to WP, starting at N30 at L, ending
N20 at R, reversing position of front band and all
the shapings, including short rows for V neck.
At the same time work buttonholes on rs2, 14, 26,
38, 50, 62 and 74. (See Notes at start.) They are
worked on the second and third r of the cable.

SLEEVES (both alike)
CO 'e' wrap 42sts. Work 16rs of border pattern
and 66rs plain knitting, increasing both ends every
6th r 12 times to RC72. K 10rs. 66sts, RC82.
Shape armhole as for back. 44sts, RC94.
K 8rs straight. RC102.
Decrease 1st both ends of next and alt rs 10 times.
Use the triple transfer tool, moving 3sts 1st in. Push
empty N back to NWP. K 1r. 24sts, RC122. COff.

MAKING UP

First join shoulder seams on machine: Push up 12
Ns. With right sides of garment together pick up
one set of shoulder sts. K 1r T10. COff with latch
tool. Pick up and finish second set of shoulder sts
the same. Pin out each pie   l give a light
pressing. Do not press border pattern, but lightly
steam, holding iron immediately above work over
a damp cloth if necessary.
Separate the two plies of MY and use a single ply
for sewing up.
Slip-stitch the sides of pocket tops to fronts,
keeping to stitch line.
Slip-stitch pocket lining in place.
Mattress-stitch front bands in place, matching
markers at commencement of 'V' neck shaping and
at shoulders.
Graft band at centre back and mattress-stitch to
neckline below the cast off row.
Mark centre of sleeve top. Run a length of yarn
along cast off row and gather.
Pin sleeve to armhole, matching shapings and
having centre of sleeve top at shoulder seam.
Adjust gathers to fit and mattress-stitch to armhole.
Mattress-stitch body and underarm seams.
Press seams, steaming all border seams.
Finally, sew on buttons to match buttonholes.

· · · · · · · · · · · · · · · · ·

Intarsia Jacket

● ● ● ● ● ● ● ● ● ● ● ● ● ● ● ● ● ●

Follow the knitting instructions for the plain jacket,
reading the colour chart for the intarsia design,
reversing the front and the pocket lining design for
the right front. The contrast yarns are used double.
Use in lengths of no more than 2m/2yd 6in.
Where contrast is only 2sts it is simpler to Swiss
darn. The instruction book for your intarsia
carriage gives full operating details. If you have
never worked this technique before, have a trial
run before embarking on the real thing. Consider
enlarging the chart for ease of working.

SIMPLE SHAPES, SMALL REPEATS

THESE ALL-OVER DESIGNS are from an ever-growing library of knitted samples. If someone wants a sweater quickly, the knitting machine can soon be in action if you have a collection of punchcards or mylar sheets to choose from, and it is even better if you also have a selection of basic shapes ready to adapt to size, in diagram form or on a charting device. Simple designs are easily organised into workable repeats; as you see from the drawings, these designs were constructed directly onto the graph paper from which the working punchcard or mylar sheet was made.

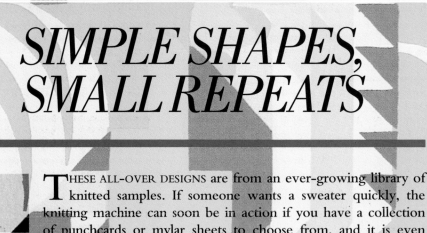

1   A browse through a book of Art Deco designs inspired this sail motif. The graded curve is squared off, and the large gaps between the motifs are filled to avoid long floats

2   The original intention was to develop a double-bed jacquard design but, I wanted to work in cotton, which would have given a heavier fabric than required so I used single-bed Fair Isle. From the design that resulted (Cubes), I also developed the two colour design 'Triangles'. Little stitch patterns can rise to great heights with an inspired use of colour, or colour and texture

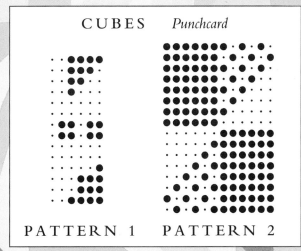

CUBES *Punchcard*

PATTERN 1   PATTERN 2

Pattern 1: *Border pattern. This is a 6st×14r repeat. The section shown is sufficient for the mylar sheet; repeat over 24sts×42rs for a punchcard*

Pattern 2: *Main pattern. This is a 12st×16r repeat. The section shown is sufficient for the electronic. Repeat over 24sts×32rs for a punchcard, remembering to begin and end the card with a double row of punched holes to join*

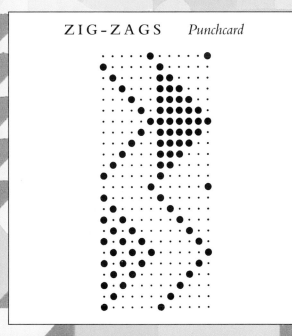

ZIG-ZAGS *Punchcard*

A 12st×24r repeat, all that is needed for the electronic machines. Punchcard users will need to punch 2 repeats, giving 24sts×48rs, beginning and ending the card with a double row of punched holes to join

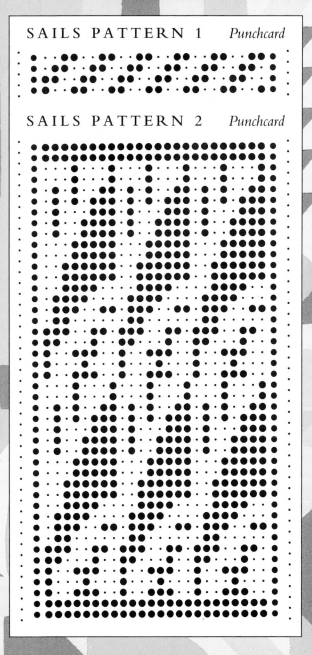

SAILS PATTERN 1 *Punchcard*

SAILS PATTERN 2 *Punchcard*

Pattern 1: *This is a 4st×4r repeat. Punchcard users need to punch a minimum of 32rs. Electronics need only mark 4st×4rs*

Pattern 2: *The pattern unit here is 24st×20rs. Punchcard users need to punch 40rs, plus the double rows of holes at each end of the card for joining. Electronic users need only one unit on the mylar sheet*

Background illustrations taken from *Abstract Art, Patterns and Designs*, Bracken Books. These are designs from 'Kaleidoscope' by A. and M.P. Verneuil (1925), here introduced by Steven Calloway.

Cubes

This design was first knitted using only the cube pattern, and in only two colours. It looked good. But the extra detail added in here at wrist and waist, and the little touch of detail at the shoulder, make it altogether more interesting. Knitted here in soft cotton, it looks equally good in pure wool or wool mixtures

. . . .

Sails

Fine cotton chenille combines well with soft cotton to give a rich fabric with luxurious interest. No ribs to knit here; reverse stocking stitch delineates hems, yoke and neckline

• • • • • • • • • • • • •

Cubes

YARN
Rowan Soft Cotton 'Sea Breeze' 4-ply equivalent.
1kg/36oz = 3950m/4345yd
1×350gm/12oz cone shade 549, dove grey; MY.
150gm/5½oz shade 559, campion; contrast col 1.
150gm/5½oz shade 560, bronze; contrast col 2.
Sweater uses all but a few metres of these yarns.

MACHINE
Standard punchcard or electronic with ribber.

TENSION
MT7, giving 33sts and 38rs to a 10cm/4in washed square.

MEASUREMENTS
Length: 63cm/25in; chest: 116cm/46in; sleeve length: 52cm/21in after washing.

NOTE   Body and sleeves are started on WY. Ribs are knitted last and decreases are made as body sections are joined to them on the machine. Shoulders and sleeves are also joined on the machine. Neckline is shaped using holding position and neckband is attached on the machine. When WY is used, 8rs are knitted before changing to main knitting, or when finishing knitting. WY is removed when knitting is finished.

COLOUR SEQUENCE
Border pattern:
2rs M.
2rs col 2. Set pattern 1.
Patt 1 colour sequence:
4rs M/1 FI.
2rs M SS.
2rs M/2 FI.
2rs M SS.
4rs M/1 FI (pattern 1 ends).
2rs col 2.
2rs M.
Main pattern, patt 2:
8rs M/1, 8rs M/2 throughout.

BACK
CO WY 190sts. K several rs ending CAR.
K border pattern. RC22 CAR.
Change to patt 2 and K to RC114. CAR.
COff 16sts at beg next 2rs.
K to RC202 CAR. Make note of pattern row number.
Shape back neck:
Set carr to HP.
Push all Ns at L of centre O and 14 at R to HP.
K to L.
Push last N knitted to HP. K to R.
Push 5 more Ns at L to HP. K to L.
Push last N knitted to HP. K to R.
Push 3 more Ns at L to HP. K to L.
Push last N knitted to HP. K to R.
Repeat last 2rs twice more. RC212.
Leave 46sts at R on WY for shoulder.
Using transfer tool replace 65sts at L to WP (14 remain at HP at L of centre O).
With carr set to hold, to slip/part/free-move, and to select needles, reset pattern on noted pattern row number from R. to L.
Finish L shoulder to match R.
K1r T7 MY on centre 66sts. Leave on WY.

FRONT
Work as for back to RC184. Make note of pattern row number.
Shape front neck:
Set carr to HP.
Push all Ns at L of centre O and 7Ns at R to HP.
K to L.
Push last N knitted to HP. K to R.
Push 2Ns at L to HP. K to L.
Push last N knitted to HP. K to R.

Repeat last 2rs once more.

Continue knitting, putting 1N at neck edge to HP on every r 19 times.

K 3rs straight. RC212.

Using transfer tool replace 72sts at L to WP (7 remain at HP at L of centre O).

Reset pattern on noted row number, method as for back, and finish L shoulder to match R.

K 1r T7 MY on centre 66sts. Leave on WY.

SLEEVES (both alike)

CO WY 98sts. Follow pattern sequence as for body, at the same time increasing at both ends every 4th r 36 times. K 8rs straight. RC152.

Mark each end of r with a length of coloured yarn.

K to RC166 CAR.

K last 6rs of patt 1 RC172. Leave on WY.

JOIN GARMENT AT SHOULDERS

Push 46Ns to WP.

Right sides of garment together, pick up 1 set of shoulder sts from WY onto Ns.

Pick up matching shoulder sts onto corresponding Ns.

K 1r MY T10.

COff using the latch tool.

JOIN SLEEVES TO ARMHOLES

Push 170 Ns to WP.

With right side of sleeve facing, pick up the sts at top of sleeve from WY. With wrong side of garment facing, shoulder seam at centre O, and underarm at N85 each side, leaving the CO sts free, pick up evenly along armhole edge approx

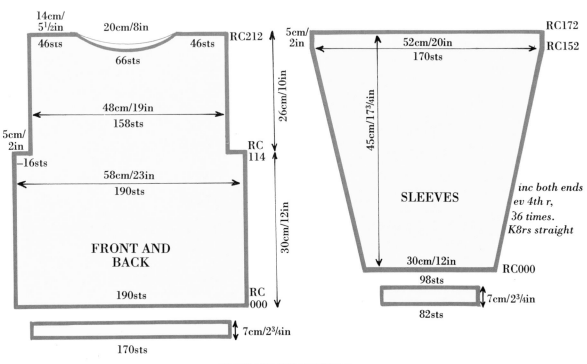

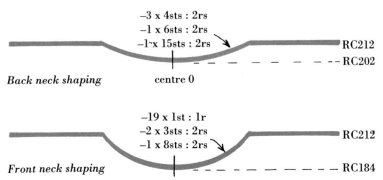

NECK SHAPING DETAIL

−3 x 4sts : 2rs
−1 x 6sts : 2rs
−1 x 15sts : 2rs

RC212
RC202

Back neck shaping   centre 0

−19 x 1st : 1r
−2 x 3sts : 2rs
−1 x 8sts : 2rs

RC212
RC184

Front neck shaping

2sts in from edge and keeping to the same line of sts. Bring Ns to HP as you do this.
Weave in ends (see Techniques).
K1r T10. COff using the latch tool.

BODY WELTS

Push up 160 Ns on both needlebeds and arrange Ns for a 2×1 rib (refer to your handbook for method). CO in col 2, and work circular rs ending CAR. RC000, change to MY. K 35rs T2/2, 1r T5/5 CAR.
Transfer ribber sts to MB.
With wrong side of body section facing, pick up sts from WY at waistline, decreasing 20sts evenly across the work by putting 2sts on a needle as necessary and avoiding any N with 2sts already on it. Bring Ns out to HP as you do this.
K 1r T10 and COff using the latch tool.

CUFFS

Push up 82Ns and work the same as body welts,

decreasing the bottom of the sleeve by 16sts when joining to the cuff.

NECKBAND

Back: Push up 70Ns. Follow welt instructions, but at RC000 work 4rs T1/1, 4rs T2/2, 4rs 2·/2·. Transfer ribber sts to MB. K 1r ss T7. With wrong side of back facing, pick up 66 neckline sts from WY onto corresponding Ns, and 2sts from the gap at each side. K 1r T10. COff loosely behind sinkers, using a transfer tool.
Front: Push up 72Ns and work as for back, picking up 3sts from gap at each side.

MAKING UP

Damp press garment omitting ribs. Steam ribs without pressing. Mattress-stitch welts, neckband and body seams, backstitch sleeve seams, matching coloured markers. Press seams, omitting ribs.

. . . .

$\mathcal{S}$ails

●●●●●●●●●●●●●●●●●●●●●●●

YARN
Rowan Soft Cotton 'Sea Breeze' 4-ply equivalent.
1kg/36oz = 3950m/4345yd.
1 350gm/12oz shade 557, forget-me-not; MY.
Rowan Fine Cotton Chenille.
1kg/36oz = 3200m/3520yd.
2×250gm/8oz cones shade 391, gorse; contrast yarn.
Sweater uses 300gm/9oz cotton, and 370gm/13oz chenille.

MACHINE
Standard punchcard or electronic without ribber.

TENSION
MT8, giving 30sts and 37rs to a 10cm/4in washed square.

MEASUREMENTS
Length: 61cm/24in; chest: 112cm/44in; sleeve length: 51cm/20in.

NOTE   The horizontal bands of blue in this tunic-style sweater are knitted in reverse stocking stitch, which entails turning the work. Instructions are given for using waste yarn to do this, but you can use a garter bar to turn the knitting. If your machine has a garter carriage you can substitute garter stitch, adding an extra 4 rows. You will notice there is a row of MY worked before turning, and again after turning. This is to prevent the contrast showing as a 'wrong' side row.

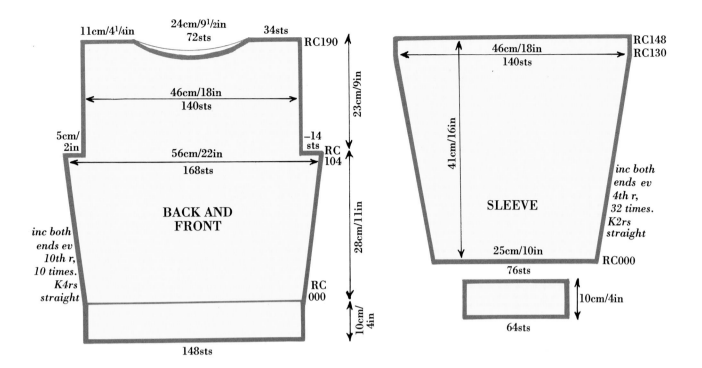

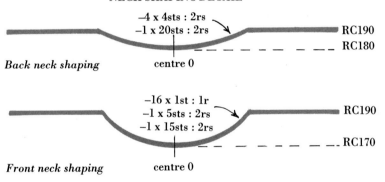

NECK SHAPING DETAIL

−4 x 4sts : 2rs
−1 x 20sts : 2rs
RC190
RC180

Back neck shaping

centre 0

−16 x 1st : 1r
−1 x 5sts : 2rs
−1 x 15sts : 2rs
RC190
RC170

Front neck shaping

centre 0

BACK

CO WY 168sts. K several rs ending CAR.
With MY K 1r T9, 8rs T4, 1r T9, 8rs T4, 1r T9.
Break yarn. K several rs WY and release from
machine.
Turn work and with right side facing replace last r
in MY onto the needles. Fold work up on the
loose row and replace the first r MY onto
corresponding Ns to form a hem. CAL, K 1r MY
setting r1 of patt 1 as you do so.
Join in contrast and K 16rs FI, T8. K 1r MY, ss.
Join in WY, K several rs, release from machine.
Turn work, and with right side facing replace sts
onto Ns.
K 8rs ss MY, T6.
Join in WY, K several rs, release from machine.
Turn work, and with wrong side facing replace sts
onto Ns.

With CAL and MY, K 1r T8 setting patt 2. CAR,
RC000.
Join in contrast. Increase at both ends every 10th r,
10 times, K to RC104. 168sts.
Shape armholes:
COff 14sts at beg next 2rs. 140sts. K to RC140.
Turn work as before, knitting 6rs MY T6 when
right side of work is facing.
Turn work. Wrong side facing. CAL, K 1r MY
T8, setting patt 1. Reset RC to 148.★ K to
RC180. CAR.
Shape back neck:
Make a note of the pattern row number. Set carr
to HP.
Bring to HP all Ns to L of centre O, and 19 to R.
K to L.
Bring last N knitted to HP. K to R.
Bring 3 Ns at L to HP. K to L.

Bring last N knitted to HP. K to R.
Repeat last 2rs 3 times more. RC190. 34sts rem at WP.
Break yarns. Join in WY. K several rs. Release from machine.
Replace Ns 20 to 70 at L to WP using transfer tool.
Set pattern on noted row. CAR.
★★Set carr to HP and to slip/part/free-move.
Reset patt from R to L.
Reset RC and finish L side to match R.

NECKBAND

Push all empty Ns to NWP. Pick up two strands yarn from gap at either side of neckline (76sts), and with MY, carr set for ss, K 1r T8, 8rs T6, 4rs T8, 3rs T6, 1r T10. COff using the latch tool.

FRONT

Work as for back to ★. K to RC170.
Shape front neck:
Make a note of the pattern row number. Set carr to HP.
Bring to HP all Ns to L of centre O, and 14Ns to R. K to L.
Bring last N knitted to HP. K to R.
Bring 4Ns at L to HP. K to L.
Bring last N knitted to HP. K to R.
Bring 1N at neck edge to HP on every r 16 times.
RC190. 34sts rem at WP.
Finish as for back.
Replace Ns 15 to 70 at L to WP using transfer tool, and finish as for back from ★★.

SLEEVES (both alike)

CO 64sts. Follow instructions for back, but K the 16rs patt 1 on T6, and increase 12 sts before setting pattern 2 as follows:
Cuff is on WY after knitting 8rs MY. Push up 6Ns either side (76Ns) and with wrong side of cuff facing replace sts onto Ns, increasing 12 sts evenly across the work (see Techniques).

With CAL and MY K 1r T8, setting patt 2.
RC000.
Increasing at both ends every 4th r, K to RC130. 140sts.
Mark each end of r with coloured yarn. K 18rs. RC148.
K several rs WY, release from machine.

JOIN GARMENT AT SHOULDERS

Push 34Ns to WP.
Right sides of garment together, pick up 1 set of shoulder sts from WY onto Ns.
Pick up matching shoulder sts onto corresponding Ns.
K 1r MY T10.
COff using latch tool.

JOIN SLEEVES TO ARMHOLE

Push 140Ns to WP.
With right side of sleeve facing pick up the sts at top of sleeve from WY. With wrong side of garment facing, shoulder seam at centre O, and underarm at N70 each side, leaving the CO sts free, pick up evenly along armhole edge approx 2sts in from edge and keeping to the same line of sts. Bring Ns to HP as you do this. Weave in ends (see Techniques).
K 1r T10. COff using latch tool.

MAKING UP

To keep the embossed look of the chenille, do not press garment. After backstitching the seams and the underarm, COff from marker to armhole seam, press seams very lightly. Finally, press the hems and lightly steam the bands of MY on the body, omitting the neckband. Let the neckband roll over naturally, slipstitch the ends together and catch-stitch it to the garment at the shoulders.

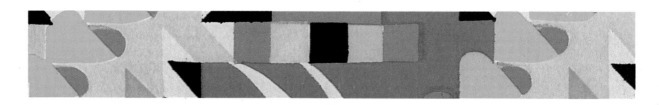

Zig-Zags

A basic sweater made special by using chenille as the contrast yarn. This and the row of 'broken' triangles give a simple pattern added depth.

You could use cotton and chenille in the same colour range to produce a lovely shadow effect, as the samples show

. . . .

Zig-Zags

YARN
Rowan Soft Cotton 'Sea Breeze' 4-ply equivalent.
1kg/36oz = 3950m/4345yd.
1×350gm/12oz cone shade 522, ecru; MY.
Rowan Fine Cotton Chenille.
1kg/36oz = 3200m/3520yd.
1×250gm/8oz cone shade 396, maple.
Sweater uses all but a few metres of both yarns.

MACHINE
Standard punchcard or electronic with ribber.

TENSION
MT8, giving 30sts and 34rs to a 10cm/4in washed square.

MEASUREMENTS
Length: 62cm/25in; chest: 116cm/46in; sleeve length: 52cm/21in.

NOTE   See note for Cubes design.

BACK
CO WY 174sts. K several rs ending CAL.
Join in MY, T8, set r1 of pattern from L to R.
RC000, join in contrast and K FI to RC102.
COff 15sts at beg next 2rs. K to RC182. CAR.
Make note of patt r number.
Shape neck:
Set carr to HP.
Bring all Ns to L of centre O and 15Ns to R of O to HP. K to L.
Bring last N knitted at L to HP. K to R.
Bring 5Ns at L to HP. K to L.
Bring last N knitted to HP. K to R.
Bring 3Ns at L to HP. K to L.
Bring last N knitted to HP. K to R.
Repeat last 2rs once more. RC190. 42sts at WP. CAR.

Break yarns. Join in WY. K several rs on 42sts at WP. Release from machine. Leave CAR.
Push empty Ns to NWP. Replace Ns 16-72 at L to WP using transfer tool.
Reset pattern card or mylar sheet on noted r number.
Set carr for HP and slip/part/free-move, and set pattern from R to L. Reset RC and finish L side to match R side.
Set carr for ss and K 1r MT8 on 60 neckline sts.
Break yarn. Join in WY, K several rs and release from machine.

FRONT
Work as for back to RC168. Make a note of patt r number. Shape the neck in the same method, starting with all Ns to L of centre O and 5Ns at R at HP, and 1N more to HP as you K back.
5Ns to HP on next r, and 1 more to HP as you K back, then 1N to HP at neck edge every r 18 times. RC190. 42sts at WP. CAR.
Finish L side to match R side, and leave neckline sts on 1r MY and several rs WY as before.

SLEEVES   (both alike)
CO WY 90sts. Work as for back to RC000. K FI, increasing both ends every 4th r 33 times. K 4rs straight. RC136. Mark each end of r with a length of coloured yarn. K to RC154. CAR.
K several rs WY. Release from machine.

JOIN GARMENT AT SHOULDERS
Follow instructions for Cubes design, working on 42Ns.

JOIN SLEEVES TO ARMHOLES
Push 156Ns to WP, and follow instructions for Cubes.

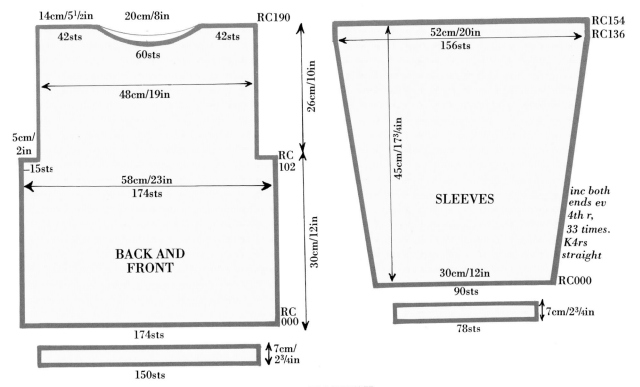

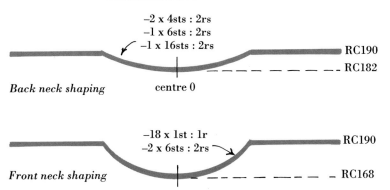

WELTS, CUFFS AND NECKBAND

Follow the instructions for Cubes but using MY only, decreasing 24sts on each body welt, and 12sts for each cuff.

Neckband:

Push up 64Ns on both needlebeds. Follow CO method in Cubes design then K 12rs T2/2, 1r T5/5, 12rs T2/2. Transfer ribber sts to MB, K 1r ss T8. Finish as for Cubes.

MAKING UP

Pressing garment body is optional; leave un-pressed if you want to retain the embossed look of the chenille. Lightly steam ribs and neckband only before backstitching underarm, COff from marker to armhole seam, mattress-stitching ribs, and backstitching main knitting.

Fold neckband in on loose row and slipstich in place. Lightly press seams.

SLIP-STITCH SWEATERS

THESE TWO SWEATERS combine and develop some of the stitch patterns created in Chapter 4. The stitch structure lends itself well to geometric patterns but imposes stylisation on organic forms. This has an attraction of its own, reminiscent of cross-stitch needlework designs.

The Little Birds design is reversed and counterchanged to produce a more fluid design. The original sample looked rather aggressive, in fact appeared to be squawking angrily! It was a simple matter to remove the lower beak from the design to produce a more pleasant expression on a happier bird.

A sweater using the Little Birds design, the ribs knitted in background colour, is attractive enough, but it is interesting to combine designs, and perhaps to have more than one contrast colour. It entails more work in the planning stage, since the different designs need to be sampled together in various ways to see which combinations work best, and also to see how they will fit into the measurements of a proposed sweater.

Different patterns in this technique can produce dramatically different measurements – the wings of the bird, for example, open up the pattern lengthways, resulting in less rows to a given measurement than the seed-stitch pattern does in the same yarn.

It is much more effective to use lightweight yarns. The 100% Pure New Wool used for Little Birds gives a finer knitted fabric than the usual Shetland yarn. It washes and presses well, becoming soft and flexible, and is perfect for this technique. The yarn for Windmills is dramatically lightweight. The contrast is a fine cotton slub, which, combined with the soft and light main yarn, produces a sweater with an airy lightness and a crunchy, crêpy texture.

It is possible to shape the neckline on the machine while knitting in this technique, but I prefer the cut-and-sew method used here. I avoided this method for years, being too apprehensive to take scissors to knitting. It was not until I saw it demonstrated that I realised how appropriate it is to certain knitting techniques. It has taught me to have a more flexible attitude: never dismiss any technique without trying it first. It is now a method I use regularly because it gives such a perfect finish, and I very much enjoy working it. If you have never done it before, knit a sample to make sure you fully understand the method. The details are in the Little Birds pattern.

1 This sample was worked to see whether the box pattern would look right at the neckline, and also to calculate the number of rows needed for the stocking stitch backing of the neck facing. The machine stitch to secure the neckline stitches was also tested on this piece

2 Here the three stitch patterns for the Windmill sweater are combined to see whether the combination is satisfactory. I decided the windmill looked better as a motif than an all-over design, and that I preferred the box pattern to delineate the sleeve as it does in the Little Birds design. So the main part of the sleeve is knitted in the background grid pattern, which I have called seed stitch

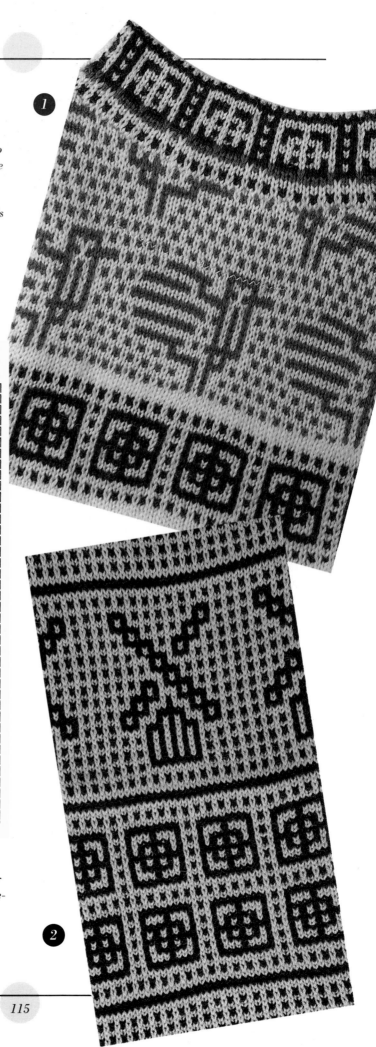

LITTLE BIRDS *Mylar sheet*

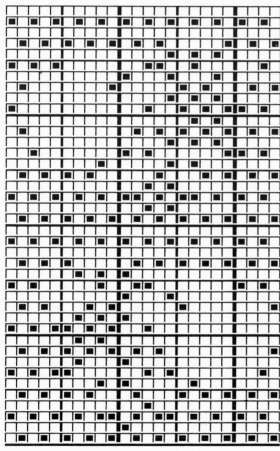

These pattern sheets are for electronic machines. The double length (elongation) and the negative switches or buttons must be used. Punchcard users need the double-length lever in action so that each row is knitted twice, but to obtain the negative image will need to punch out the background, NOT the pattern

Little Birds

Shetland yarn comes in many lovely colours, but blue on white was a deliberate choice, combined with this slip stitch technique the design is reminiscent of the old willow pattern.

. . . .

Windmills

Although the yarn for this sweater contains just a small proportion of wool, the cellular structure of the knitting makes it light and warm. Press only the seams, to maintain this airy quality.

. . . .

Little Birds

YARN
Texere 100% Pure New Wool Shetland 2/10,
3-ply equivalent, 50gm/2oz = 270m/297yd approx.
1×500gm/17oz cone natural; MY.
1×500gm/17oz cone denim; col 1.
100gm/3oz navy; col 2.
Sweater uses 320gm/11oz MY, 200gm/7oz col 1,
100gm/3oz col 2.

MACHINE
Standard punchcard or electronic with ribber and
optional single-bed colour changer. If a colour
changer is not being used the yarns must be
changed manually at the right side of the machine
every two rows. The instructions are given
assuming use of a colour changer.

TENSION
MT7, giving 36sts and 30rs to a 10cm/4in square
after washing. Because 2 passes of the carriage are
necessary for one complete row in this slip-stitch
pattern, the row counter will record double the
number of rows knitted, eg the 60rs to be
measured on the tension square will record as 120
on the row counter.

MEASUREMENTS
Length: 64cm/25in; chest 112cm/44in; sleeve
length: 50cm/19¾in after garment is washed.

NOTES   It is a good idea to knit all the ribs first,
leaving them on WY. The number of Ns are then
increased for the main knitting, the extra sts being
made as the rib is replaced on the machine (see
Techniques). The pattern is a slip-stitch mosaic
pattern knitted with the carriage set to slip in both
directions. For punchcard machines it is the
background which is punched out: the pattern is the
unpunched area of the card. Each row of the
card is knitted twice, so the double-length lever or

button must be used. Electronic machines are set
for double length and negative. The first pattern
row can be set either by knitting in MY, or by
setting the carriage to slip/part/free-move/empty.
After ribbing it is done by the first method, but
when changing from the border pattern to the main
pattern it is done by the second method as follows:
Border pattern ends with 2rs MY (natural).
Change to main pattern, lock or set on first row.
With no yarn in feeder, and carriage set to
slip/part/free-move/empty, select r1 of new
pattern as follows:
Colour changer: Carr is at L. Slip it across to R,
and then set it to select the pattern. Move carr back
to L, pattern is selected.
Manual: The pattern is selected in the same way,
but the carr starts from the R because the colours
will be changed manually at the right side of the
machine. Remember that the pattern on the card
or sheet always starts with 2rs contrast and must
end with 2rs MY/background. If you need to
unpick rows of knitting for any reason it is better
to start knitting again on the first of the two
contrast rows.
Neckline: This is worked using the cut-and-sew
method. Full instructions are given in the pattern.

RIBS
If you are using a single-bed colour changer
remove the arm while you knit the rib, because the
welt is knitted in stripes and it is easier to change
the colours at the left (manually) when using the
ribber.
Arrange Ns for 1×1 rib. Using col 1, CO, K
circular rs ending CAR.
RC000, T 1/1. K to L.
Changing cols manually, K 2rs M, 2rs col 1 to
RC36. K 1r T5/5.
Transfer ribber sts to empty Ns of MB.
K several rs WY and release from machine.

BACK and FRONT (both alike)

Bring 170Ns to WP on both beds. Work rib as above. Bring 198Ns to WP on MB and hang the last r of rib onto the Ns, increasing 28sts evenly across the Ns (see Techniques).

CAL RC000 border pattern locked or set on first r. With MY in feeder, K 2rs, setting r1 of border pattern on 2nd r. K in pattern, 2rs col 2, 2rs M, to RC30, ending 2rs MY. CAL.

Lock Little Birds pattern on r1. Set pattern with no yarn in feeder as described in notes. (Don't forget to turn RC back 2rs afterwards.)

K in pattern 2rs col 1, 2rs MY to RC196.

COff 18sts at beg of next 2rs.

K to RC350. 4 complete patts. Mark centre O with a length of coloured yarn.

Now leave 36sts at L, 90sts at centre, and 36sts at R separately on WY.

Work another piece the same.

PREPARE NECKLINE FOR NECKBAND

Join *one* shoulder on machine:

Push 36Ns to WP. With right sides of garment together, pick up one set of shoulder sts onto Ns.

Pick up matching shoulder sts onto same Ns. K 1r MY T10. COff using latch tool.

Steam-press neckline area and shoulder seam. Mark centre front 6cm/2½in below coloured marker on last row; centre back 4cm/1½in below coloured marker.

You can now work directly onto the garment (or make a cardboard template if preferred). Using a soft pencil (5B) or tacking thread, mark a horizontal line 10cm/4in centred on front marking. Similarly, mark a line 15cm/6in on the back. Continue the ends of each line to the neck edge in a gentle curve. If you have a French curve or similar, use it to do this, but a large plate will do just as well. Without stretching the knitting, work a double line of zig-zag machine sts, or hand backstitch, along the planned line. Cut away the surplus knitted fabric inside the stitching.

NECKBAND

The number of Ns is calculated by laying the prepared neckline along the machine with shoulder seam at centre O, and without stretching the knitting. CO WY 170sts. (This gives 14 border pattern repeats plus 1st at each end for seaming.) K several

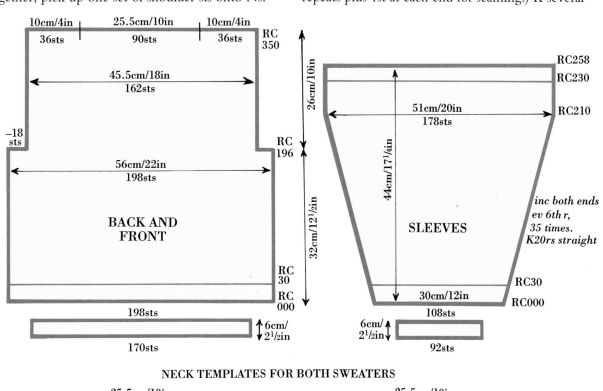

NECK TEMPLATES FOR BOTH SWEATERS

rs ending CAR. Break yarn.

With nylon cord, K 1r T9 CAL.

With MY T10 K 1r.

Border pattern set or locked on first row.

T7, set 1st r border pattern from R to L.

RC000, K in pattern 2rs col 2, 2rs MY to RC28 changing tension as follows:

8rs T7, 8rs T6, 6rs T5, 6rs T4.

Break col 2. Carr set for ss. Using MY, K 1r T9.

K 20rs ss, changing tension as follows:

5rs T4, 5rs T5★, 5rs T6, 5rs T7, K 1r T10.

Now take the garment, and with the right side up, lay it over the MB of the machine so that the neckline faces you. Have the shoulder seam at centre O, centre necks at N42 each side of centre O, and other shoulder seam at N84. It does not matter if the sinkers come through the fabric. Push the Ns through the fabric above the stitched rs, bringing them no further forward than UWP. Pick up the sts on T10 from the bottom of the hem. The sts *must* rest in the latches. Close the latches (use the little cleaning brush provided with your machine). Now carefully push the Ns back evenly, a little at a time (making sure that no sts go behind the latches) until they all rest against the knitting. Pull them through the knitted fabric, and then bring this forward to hang down in front of the machine, lifting off any fabric that rests on the sinkers as you do so. The wrong side will face you. Check that all the sts are in the Ns and bring them out to HP.

T10, MY in the feeder, K the Ns back to WP.

Cast off loosely around the sinkers (see Techniques).

Carefully remove nylon cord: the WY will fall away from the work.

Close the second shoulder seam to match the first.

SLEEVES (both alike)

Bring 92sts to WP on both beds. Work rib as before. Bring 108Ns to WP on MB, and hang the last r of rib onto the Ns, increasing 16sts evenly across the Ns (see Techniques).

Work border pattern, then Little Birds pattern as for back to RC230 (2½ complete patterns), at the same time increasing at both ends of every 6th r until there are 178sts (at RC210).

CAL change to border pattern, setting the first row without yarn in feeder as given in notes. K 2rs col 2, 2rs MY to RC258. Pattern ends with 2rs MY. K several rs WY and release from machine.

JOIN SLEEVES TO ARMHOLES

Bring 178Ns to WP. With right side of sleeve facing, pick up 178sts from last r of sleeve.

With wrong side of body facing, shoulder at centre O, underarms (excluding 18 COff sts) at N89 each side pick up 178sts evenly keeping to the same line of sts, 2sts in from the edge. Weave in ends (see Techniques). K 1r T10, COff with the latch tool.

MAKING UP

After finishing off all ends, the garment should be washed by hand using washing-up liquid to remove oil. Squeeze out excess moisture, or spin in a closed pillowcase and dry flat. Damp-press garment and neckband excluding all ribs. Steam ribs by holding iron close to garment but not pressing. With MY, backstitch COff sts at underarm to edge of border pattern at top of sleeve. Close neckband seam using mattress-stitch, and mattress-stitch all ribs and seams. Damp-press seams, steam rib seams.

· · · · · · · · · · · ·

Windmills

● ● ● ● ● ● ● ● ● ● ● ● ● ● ● ● ● ●

YARN

Celandine Sara for machine knitting, 70% Acrylic, 20% wool, 10% alpaca. 50gm/2oz = 350m/385yd. 1×350gm/12oz cone shade 10; MY.

Celandine Nibbiolo, 80% cotton, 20% nylon. 50gm/2oz = 400m/440yd. 1×250gm/9oz cone; contrast.

Sweater uses 200gm/7oz MY, 90gm/3oz contrast.

MACHINE
As for Little Birds.

TENSION
MT7, giving 30sts and 32rs to a 10cm/4in square.
See additional information in Little Birds pattern.
Tension squares should be worked for the seed
stitch pattern and the squares pattern. Knit and
measure the length of one windmill plus the stripes
bordering it. If making length adjustments on the
body take into account that the box pattern should
end with a repeat of rs 1 and 2, or at r14. In either
case this will be 2rs MY. Length adjustments can
be made in the seed stitch pattern on the yoke or
sleeve.

MEASUREMENTS
Length: 61cm/24½in; chest: 112cm/44in; sleeve
length: 50cm/17¾in.

NOTES   Read the notes for Little Birds; the method
for changing patterns is given in the instructions
which follow here.

RIBS
All ribs are worked as follows: Arrange Ns for 2×1
rib. After 3 circular rs, CAR. RC000, T2/2, K
33rs. T5/5 K 1r CAL.
Transfer ribber sts to MB. K several rs WY and
release from machine.

BACK and FRONT (both alike)
Bring 146Ns to WP on both beds. K rib as above.
Bring 168Ns to WP on MB. Hang the last r of rib
onto Ns, increasing 22sts evenly across work.
RC000, CAL T5: K 2rs C, 2rs MY, 2rs C.
Pattern 1 set or locked on r1, MY in feeder, T7, K
to R. K to L setting pattern.
Carr set for slip stitch, K 2rs C, 2rs MY to RC200
(4 complete patterns).
K first 2rs pattern again. RC204.
Change to ss and T5: casting off 15sts at beg of
next 2rs, K 2rs C, 2rs MY, 2rs C. RC210.
Windmill, pattern 2, set or locked on r1, MY in
feeder, T7, K to R. K to L setting pattern.
Carr set for slip stitch K 2rs C, 2rs MY to RC266
(1 complete pattern).
Change to ss and T5: K 2rs C, 2rs MY, 2rs
C. RC272.
Pattern 3 set or locked on R1, MY in feeder, T7,
K to R. K to L setting pattern.

WINDMILL   *Mylar sheet*

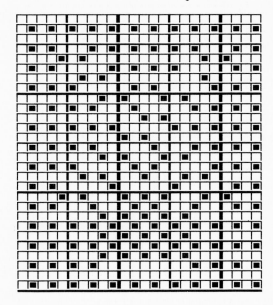

BOX PATTERN   *Mylar sheet*

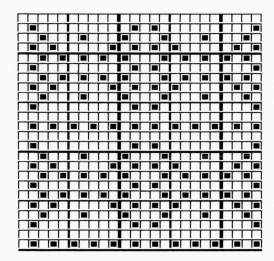

*Box pattern. The first 14 rows are used for border
pattern of the Little Birds design, and on the sleeve
borders of Windmills. Punchcards will need to repeat
the first 12 rows again, giving a 36 row card when
knitting the main part of Windmills*

SEED STITCH   *Mylar sheet*

*Seed stitch: Punchcard users need to punch a
minimum of 32 rows*

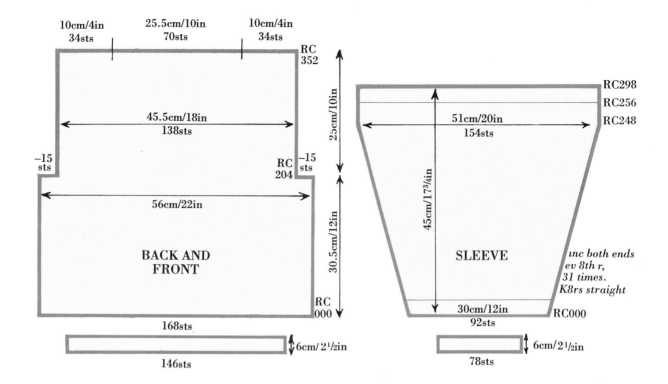

Carr set for slip stitch, K 2rs C, 2rs MY to RC352.
Mark centre O on knitting with a length of
coloured yarn. Now leave 34sts at L, 70sts at
centre, and 34sts at R separately on WY.
Work another piece the same.

PREPARE NECKLINE FOR NECKBAND
Follow instructions for Little Birds, but DO NOT
PRESS the knitting.

NECKBAND
CO WY 158sts, giving 13 box pattern repeats plus
1st each end for seaming.
Follow instructions for Little Birds to ★, K 10rs T6.
Attach the neckband and close the second shoulder
as for Little Birds.

SLEEVES
Bring 78sts to WP on both beds. Work rib as before.
Bring 92Ns to WP on MB and hang the last r of
rib onto Ns increasing 14sts evenly across Ns (see
Techniques).
Increasing at both ends every 8th r until there are
154sts (31 times at RC248) work in pattern as
follows:
RC000, ★CAL, T5, K 2rs C, 2rs MY, 2rs C.
Set or lock patt 1 on r1 as before.

K 14rs in pattern ending CAL, RC36.
Carr set to ss T5 K 2rs C, 2rs MY, 2rs C★.
Set or lock patt 3 on r1 as before, T7, K in pattern
to RC256.
Repeat from ★to★. RC298 K 1r MY T9. Leave on
several rs WY.

JOIN SLEEVES TO ARMHOLES
Bring 154Ns to WP. With right side of sleeve
facing, pick up 154sts from last r of sleeve.
With wrong side of body facing, shoulder at centre
O, underarms (excluding 15 COff sts) at N77 each
side, last ss r above Windmill design at approx
N40, pick up 154sts evenly, keeping to the same
line of sts, 2sts in from the edge.
Weave in ends (see Techniques). K 1r T10, COff
with the latch tool.

MAKING UP

After finishing off all ends, press the garment lightly
with a dry iron on a cool setting, on the wrong
side. DO NOT be tempted to use a hot iron with
steam or you will spoil the texture of the knitting.
Backstitch COff sts at underarm to edge of patt 1.
Close neckband seam using mattress stitch, and
mattress-stitch all ribs and seams. Press seams with a
cool dry iron on the wrong side of garment.

TECHNIQUES

All instruction books give basic techniques, and most knitters have learnt a few which are not to be found on the printed page. Except for the cabling and stitch re-forming, the following techniques have been passed on to me in the traditional manner: by example. I include them here because I use them constantly, for their neatness and time-saving qualities. They are easy to work, and well worth learning.

1 and 2   HAND CAST ON, 'E' WRAP

This gives a much firmer edge than the simple wrapping most machine knitters know. It is particularly useful when casting on while knitting is in progress, and can be worked from the left, as shown here, or right of the knitting. Be careful not to work it too tightly.

1   Two needles at the opposite end to the carriage are brought to HP. Make a closed loop on the end needle. Wrap the yarn under, then over both Ns, with the yarn in the latch of the end needle. Pull this back to WP, pulling the yarn through the loop to form a new stitch. The loop formed on the second needle will slide right down behind the latch.

2   Bring the next N on the R to HP. Wrap the yarn over 2Ns as before, and with the yarn in the latch of the

left needle, pull back to WP. Continue wrapping and forming a new stitch as required. Before knitting the cast-on stitches, bring the Ns out to HP, to make sure they knit properly, then hang your weights.

3 and 4   SPLIT-STITCH CAST OFF

Most knitters know how to cast off loosely with the transfer tool by taking the yarn behind the sinkers to give the finished edge more elasticity. If an even more flexible finish is needed, the stitch to be cast off can be enlarged by stretching it over two needles before pulling the yarn through as shown. The new stitch in the needle is then stretched onto the next needle and the process repeated. When the last stitch is cast off, the end of the yarn is pulled right through the stitch to secure. The work can then be lifted off the needles or removed by passing the empty carriage across the bed.

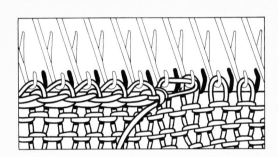

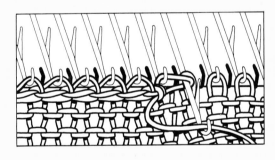

5   SECURING ENDS AT THE SIDE OF THE WORK

When a new yarn is introduced at the side of the work, the end of the old and the new yarn can be wrapped around the end needle on every other row, 3 or 4 times.

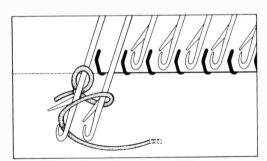

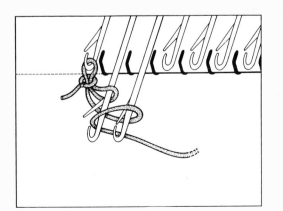

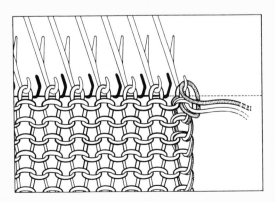

Pull the end N out to HP and knit it back to WP as you do this, if your pattern will allow. The ends can then be trimmed off. Do not use this method at the armhole edge if you plan to join to the sleeve top on the machine. The next technique is better for this purpose.

6   WEAVING ENDS ACROSS THE NEEDLES

When two garment pieces are joined on the machine, ends can be woven under and over several needles, after both garment pieces have been picked up and the needles are at holding position. Where there are a lot of ends several can be woven, alternating, on the same needles. The joining row is then knitted on the highest (ie loose) tension before casting off, the ends are then trimmed. This technique is most often used when joining sleeve top to armhole. The method would be to place the sleeve stitches on the needles first, right side facing, then, with wrong side of garment body facing, pick up evenly along the armhole edge.

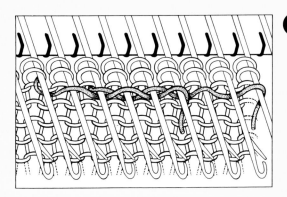

7   TWO DIFFERENT WAYS TO INCREASE THE STITCHES AFTER KNITTING THE WELT

Calculate the required number of stitches for the welt (main knitting minus, perhaps, 12sts, for example). After knitting the desired length, transfer ribber stitches to MB. K1r in MT, and leave on WY. CO for main knitting in WY and K several rs. Change to MY and K the garment piece.

To join: Hang welt onto Ns, right side of work facing. With wrong side of garment piece facing, hang the first row stitches onto Ns, putting 2 on a needle

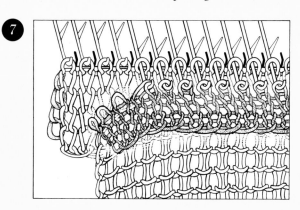

where necessary evenly across the work. The positions can be planned in advance, and to save calculation can be approximate rather than exact. K 1r T10 and cast off with the latch tool.

8   Knit the welt as before, leaving on WY. Now push up the number of Ns required for the main knitting. Pick up the welt stitches, spacing the required number of extra needles evenly across the bed, leaving them empty. Carefully pull out WY from behind knitting. Pick up the strand of yarn below each empty needle, pointing the transfer tool downwards as shown below.

9   As you turn the tool the right way up the strand of yarn will twist to form an 'e' wrap on the transfer tool. Transfer it to the empty needle. Twisting the yarn prevents a hole showing where the increase has been made.

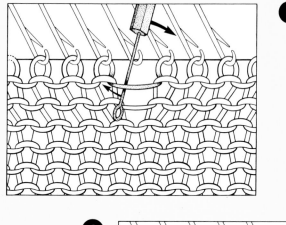

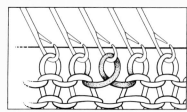

FULLY FASHIONED DECREASES

These are generally worked using the triple transfer tool. Pick up three edge stitches and transfer them two stitches in. Push the two empty needles back to NWP. This way decreases can be made on every 4th row instead of on alternate rows, and gives good styling to sleeve shaping where the sleeve is knitted down from the armhole, saving time too.

10 and 11   RE-FORMING STITCHES

The examples shown (top right) are for a rib, but the method is the same when the stitch to be re-formed flanks a cable. The stitch is dropped and allowed to run down the work. Where the lower edge is cast on, be careful not to drop the stitch too far or you will lose the edge formation. If you are re-forming two adjacent stitches, drop and work them singly. Do not pull or stretch the knitting as you work this technique.

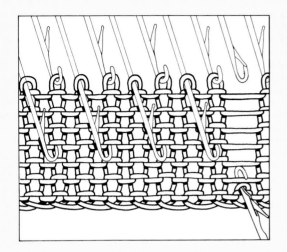

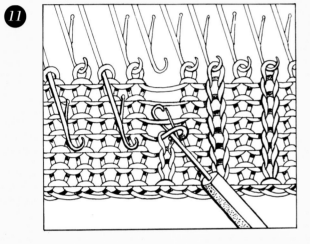

12   MAKING CABLE CROSSINGS

The example given below is for a 2 cross 2 cable, to illustrate the method. The right pair of stitches will cross over the left.

Transfer the right-hand pair to the transfer tool, holding them over towards the right and well down the shanks of the tool. Using a second transfer tool, lift off the left pair of sts, and transfer them to the two empty

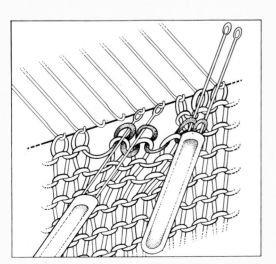

Ns at the right. Now transfer the two sts waiting at the right to the two empty Ns at the left, and the cable crossing is complete. Knit the next row carefully, perhaps bringing the cabled Ns out to HP and knitting back to WP to avoid dropped sts.

13   HOW TO MAKE A TEMPLATE FOR A CUT-AND-SEW NECKLINE

These instructions, which were used in the African Weave design, are for a standard crew neckline 20cm/8in wide. The width and depth can be altered according to your needs.

You will need cardboard, (a cereal packet will do), ruler, pencil and a French curve. You could use a dinner plate.

Front: Draw a horizontal line 20cm/8in. Mark the centre, and mark a point 8cm/3¼in immediately below this for the depth of the neck.

Using this point as centre front, draw a horizontal line 5cm/2½in wide.

Using a French curve, join the ends of the 20cm/8in line to the ends of the 5cm/2½in line to give the neckline curve.

Back: Draw as for front, changing the measurements. Neck depth: 2.5cm/1in; horizontal line at centre: 12cm 4¾in.

Cut out these shapes, and mark the measurements on them for future reference.

13b   The neckline is marked with tacking thread on the garment piece. Use the homemade template or a purchased plastic template to plan the line.

On the body side of the neckline, ie NOT the section you will cut away, work two parallel rows of machine stitching to secure the knitted fabric. Use a stretch stitch suitable for jersey fabric. If you prefer to hand stitch, use two rows of backstitch, trying not to pull the stitches too tight. Cut away surplus knitted fabric.

Press the knitting according to the yarn content, and cut away the neck along the line of tacking stitches. If you plan to join the shoulders on the machine, check that you have the correct number of shoulder stitches at each side of the neck, and secure the neck-edge stitch before cutting. This edge will then be enclosed by the circular rows of the neckband.

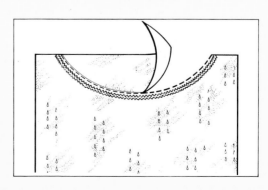

14 SWISS DARNING

You can introduce extra colour into the knitting by imitating the knitted stitch, as shown. There are examples of the technique throughout the text.

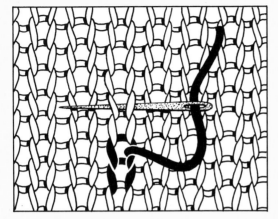

15 GRAFTING

This is an invisible method of joining two pieces of knitting, both edges generally being on waste yarn. The knitted fabric is first pressed, then a false row is worked with a length of main yarn. The yarn should be about three times as long as the sections to be joined. Try to imitate the stitch size of the original so that the join is virtually unseen. Strip away the waste yarn when finished. This technique can be used as a finish to full needle rib bands.

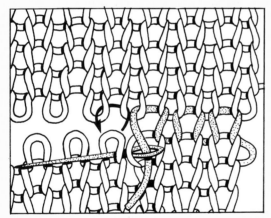

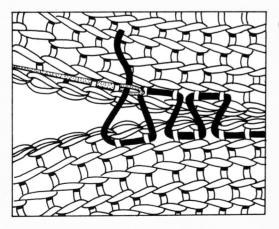

16 MATTRESS-STITCH

This is the neatest method of joining seams, and is worked from the right side of the garment. It is almost invisible, and is particularly neat for ribbed seams. The yarn is pulled tight every few stitches.

KNITTING ELASTIC

Fine elastic can be knitted into the welts if you doubt the elasticity of the yarn or if you prefer not to increase stitches for the main part of the garment after ribbing. In the latter case, cast on for the welt the number of stitches required for the main knitting.

The best elastic to use is supplied on a reel which revolves in a small plastic holder. This can be hung on the yarn mast. The yarn for the welt is threaded through the tension unit and the yarn feeder in the usual way. The elastic is *not* threaded through the tension unit, but is passed directly from its position on the mast into the feeder. Use elastic a tone darker than the knitting yarn and it will be virtually invisible, even if the colour is not an exact match.

KNITTING A TENSION SQUARE

Tension square for 200 needle machines:
Cast on 60sts in chosen tension and MY
K 20rs in stitch pattern. Record the tension on the 6th row by making the required number of holes to represent the stitch dial number. Do this by transferring stitches and leaving the empty needles at WP
K 2rs ss in contrast yarn
K 30rs in stitch pattern and MY
K Ns 21 each side of centre O by hand in contrast yarn
K 30rs in stitch pattern and MY
K 2rs ss in contrast yarn
K 20rs in stitch pattern and MY
COff loosely or leave on WY
Leave the square to relax for several hours or overnight. If the yarn is prepared 'in oil' it should be washed and allowed to dry. Press according to the yarn content.
Measuring the square: The stitch measurements are taken between the marked stitches, the row measurements between the marked rows. Use the 'Green Ruler', which is specially marked to give an accurate reading over 10cm (4in). If you are not using this device measure in the centre using an ordinary ruler. Do not measure the sides. The Green Ruler is indispensible for tuck and slip patterns where rows and stitches are difficult to count.
Chunky tension square: Knit in the same way as above, but CO 40sts. Halve the other numbers, knitting Ns 11 each side of centre O in contrast yarn on r15. The Green Ruler can be used to measure, and the reading halved.
Ribber tension square: Prepare in the same way as above, counting the needles on the main bed only, whether they have stitches on them or not, and knitting N21 at either side of centre O in contrast yarn

YARN STOCKISTS

Texere Yarns

College Mill, Barkerend Road, Bradford BD3 3AQ.

Glenora Craft Supplies, South Avondale Road, Dapto, New South Wales, Australia.

Gerald H. Whittaker Ltd/Inc, 12 Keefer Road, St Catherines, Ontario L2M7N9, Canada.

Gerald H. Whittaker Ltd/Inc, PO Box 35, 3255 Lockport Road, Niagara Falls, NY State 14305, USA.

Celandine Ltd

44 Kirkgate, Otley, West Yorkshire LS21 3HJ.

Worldwide mail order service
Rowan Yarns

Green Lane Mill, Washpit, Holmfirth, Huddersfield, West Yorkshire HD7 1RW. Mail order service available.

For overseas stockists and mail order details please contact:

AUSTRALIA: Rowan (Australia), 191 Canterbury Rd, Canterbury, Victoria 3126 Tel (03) 830 1609

BELGIUM: Hedera, Pleinstraat 68, 3001 Leuven Tel (016) 23 21 89

CANADA: Estelle Designs & Sales Ltd, Units 65/67, 2220 Midland Ave, Scarborough, Ontario M1P 3E6 Tel (416) 298 9922

DENMARK: Designer Garn, Vesterbro 33A, DK-9000 Aalborg Tel 98 13 48 24

FINLAND: Helmi-Vuorelma-Oy, Vesijarvenkatu 13, SF-15141 Lahti Tel (081) 826 831

FRANCE: Sidel, Chernin Departemental 14C, 13840 Rognes Tel (33) 42 50 15 06

GERMANY: Christoph Fritzsch GmbH, Gewerbepark Dogelmuhle, D-6367 Karben 1 Tel 06039 20/1

HOLLAND: Henk & Henrietta Beukers, Dorpsstraat 9, NL-5327 AR Hurwenen Tel 04182 1764

ICELAND: Storkurinn, Kjorgardi, Laugavegi 59, ICE-101 Reykjavik Tel (01) 18258

ITALY: La Compagnia Del Cotone, Via Mazzini 44, 1-10123 Torino Tel (011) 87 83 81

JAPAN: Diakeito Co Ltd, 2-3-11 Senba-Higashi, Minoh City, Osaka 562 Tel 0727 27 6604

MEXICO: Rebecca Pick Estambresy Tejidos Finos SA de CV, AV Michoacan 30 - A, Local 3 Esq Av Mexico, Col Hipodromo Condesa 06170, Mexico 11, DF Mexico Tel (05) 2 64 84 74

NEW ZEALAND: John Q Goldingham Ltd, PO Box 45083, Epunl Rahway, Lower Hutt Tel (04) 5674 085

NORWAY: Eureka, PO Box 357, N-1401 Ski Tel (09) 871909

SINGAPORE: The Yarn Garden, 126 Joo Seng Rd No. 07-11, Gold Pine Industrial Building, Singapore 1336 Tel 2883733

SWEDEN: Wincent, Sveavagen 94, 113 50 Stockholm Tel (08) 673 70 60

USA: Westminster Trading Corporation, 5 Northern Boulevard, Amherst, New Hampshire 03031 Tel (603) 886 5041/5043

Yorkshire Mohair Mill

Mohair Mills, Gibson Street, Bradford BD3 9TS. Worldwide mail order service.

FURTHER READING

TECHNIQUES

All Mary Weaver's books are invaluable. They are obtainable from knitting machine stockists, and from: Weaverknits, 276-8 Main Road, Sutton-at-Hone, Dartford, Kent.

Ribber Techniques Book (Brother). Available from knitting machine stockists.

Guagliumi, Susan. *Machine Knitting Hand Tooling Techniques* (Batsford)

Kinder, Kathleen. *Mosaic Floatless Fair Isle*. Available from knitting machine stockists.

Lewis, Susanna and Weissman, Julia. *A Machine Knitter's Guide to Creating Fabrics* (Sterling/Lark, New York).

Lorant, Tessa. *The Good Yarn Guide* (The Thorn Press)

Pope, Hazel. *The Machine Knitter's Handbook* (David & Charles).

Walker, Barbara. *Charted Knitting Designs* (Charles Scribner, New York)

INSPIRATION

This list is the tip of an enormous iceberg, but makes a good 'starter' for a collection of source books.

Allen, Jeanne. *The Designer's Guide to Japanese Patterns* (two books) (Thames and Hudson)

Kalter, Johannes. *The Arts and Crafts of Turkestan* (Thames and Hudson)

Noma, Seiroku. *Japanese Costume and Textile Arts* (Weatherhill/Heibonsha, New York/Tokyo)

Sayer, Chloe. *Mexican Patterns: A Design Source Book* (Studio Editions, London)

Spinhoven, Co. *Celtic Charted Designs* (Dover)

Verneuil, A. and M.P. *Abstract Art Patterns and Designs* (Bracken Books, Bestseller Publications Ltd). Bracken Books produce a list of colourful design source books

INDEX